Mastering Bitcoin and Blockchain

A Beginner's Guide to Cryptocurrencies and Decentralized Technology

Erik Schäfer Johnson

Disclaimer

Copyright © 2024 by Erik Schäfer Johnson
All rights reserved. No part of this publication may be reproduced, stored or transmitted in any form or by any means, electronic, mechanical, photocopying, recording, scanning, or otherwise without written permission from the publishers. It is illegal to copy this book, post it to a website, or distribute it by any other means without permission.

Erik Schäfer Johnson asserts the moral right to be identified as the authors of this book.

Table of Contents

Introduction

PART 1: Introduction to Cryptocurrencies and Blockchain Technology
1.1. What Are Cryptocurrencies?
1.2. The Evolution of Money
1.3. Why Cryptocurrencies Matter
1.3.1. Decentralization
1.3.2. Financial Inclusion
1.3.3. Transparency and Security
1.3.4. Low Transaction Costs and Speed
1.3.5. Hedge Against Inflation
1.3.6. Programmable Money
1.3.7. Empowerment Through Ownership
1.3.8. Potential for Global Impact

2. What is Blockchain?
2.1. How Blockchain Works
2.1.1. Creation of a Transaction
2.1.2. Verification
2.1.3. Grouping into Blocks
2.1.4. Consensus Mechanism
2.1.5. Adding the Block to the Chain
2.1.6. Immutability
2.1.7. Decentralized Storage
2.2. Key Features of Blockchain Technology

2.2.1. Decentralization
2.2.2. Transparency
2.2.3. Immutability
2.2.4. Security
2.2.5. Efficiency
2.2.6. Smart Contracts
2.2.7. Distributed Ledger
2.3. Decentralization and Its Benefits
2.3.1. What is Decentralization?
2.3.2. Benefits of Decentralization
2.3.3. Challenges of Decentralization

3. The Birth of Bitcoin
3.1. The Story of Satoshi Nakamoto
3.2. The Genesis Block and Bitcoin's Origins

PART 2: Understanding Bitcoin
4. How Bitcoin Works
4.1. Bitcoin Transactions Explained
4.2. Mining and the Creation of New Bitcoins
4.3. The Role of Nodes in the Bitcoin Network

5. Buying, Selling, and Using Bitcoin
5.1. Setting Up a Bitcoin Wallet
5.2. Exchanges: Buying and Selling Bitcoin

6. Bitcoin Security and Privacy
6.1. Protecting Your Wallet

6.2. Common Scams and How to Avoid Them
6.3. The Role of Anonymity in Bitcoin

PART 3: Blockchain Beyond Bitcoin
7. Altcoins and Their Ecosystem
7.1. What Are Altcoins?
7.3. How Altcoins Differ from Bitcoin

8. Smart Contracts and Decentralized Applications (dApps)
8.1. Introduction to Smart Contracts
8.2. Real-Life Use Cases of dApps

9. The Rise of Decentralized Finance (DeFi)
9.1. What is DeFi?
9.3. Risks and Rewards in DeFi

PART 4: Technical and Practical Insights
10. Blockchain Technology in Depth
10.1. Understanding Consensus Mechanisms
10.2. Scaling Challenges and Solutions

11. The Role of Cryptography in Blockchain
11.1. Public and Private Keys Explained
11.1.1. Asymmetric Cryptography
11.1.2. Key Generation
11.1.3. Role in Blockchain Transactions
11.1.4. Importance of Private Key Security

11.2. Hashing and Digital Signatures
11.2.3. Application in Blockchain

12. The Future of Blockchain Technology
12.1. Blockchain in Industries: Healthcare, Supply Chain, and More
12.2. Emerging Trends: NFTs, Web3, and the Metaverse

PART 5: Challenges and Opportunities
13. Regulations and Legal Implications
13.1. Global Perspectives on Cryptocurrency Regulation

14. Environmental Impact of Cryptocurrencies
14.1. Energy Consumption and Bitcoin Mining
14.2. Sustainable Blockchain Solutions

15. Investing in Cryptocurrencies
15.1. Understanding Risks and Rewards
15.2. Diversifying Your Crypto Portfolio
15.3. Long-Term Trends in Crypto Investing

PART 6: Getting Started
16. Step-by-Step Guide to Your First Bitcoin
16.1. Choosing the Right Wallet
16.2 Safely Purchasing and Storing Bitcoin

17. Building Your Knowledge and Skills
17.1. Reliable Resources for Learning More

17.2. Staying Updated in a Rapidly Changing Field

Conclusion

Introduction

In recent years, few innovations have generated as much excitement—and controversy—as Bitcoin and blockchain technology. What began as an obscure idea in a white paper written by a pseudonymous individual known as Satoshi Nakamoto has now evolved into a global phenomenon. Cryptocurrencies like Bitcoin have transformed our understanding of money, while the blockchain—the revolutionary technology underpinning these digital currencies—has paved the way for innovation in countless industries.

Yet, for many, the world of Bitcoin and blockchain remains intimidating. Headlines about market volatility, technical jargon, and stories of rapid wealth creation or devastating losses can make the topic feel inaccessible. This book aims to change that. Whether you're a complete novice curious about how Bitcoin works, a professional exploring blockchain's applications, or someone eager to understand the future of money and technology, this book is your starting point.

Why Bitcoin and Blockchain Matter

To appreciate the significance of Bitcoin and blockchain, we must first understand the problems they seek to solve. Traditional financial systems rely heavily on trusted intermediaries such as banks, payment processors, and governments.

While these institutions have played a vital role in facilitating commerce and ensuring economic stability, they also come with limitations:

High Costs: Transactions involving intermediaries often incur significant fees, particularly for cross-border payments.

Limited Access: Billions of people around the world remain unbanked or underbanked, unable to access essential financial services.

Lack of Transparency: Centralized systems are prone to corruption, inefficiencies, and opaque decision-making.

Security Risks: The centralization of financial systems makes them prime targets for hackers and data breaches.

Bitcoin was designed to address these challenges by enabling peer-to-peer transactions without relying on intermediaries. Blockchain, the underlying technology, goes even further. By offering a decentralized, transparent, and secure way to record and verify transactions, blockchain has the potential to disrupt industries far beyond finance, including supply chain management, healthcare, and voting systems.

What You'll Learn in This Book

This book provides a comprehensive introduction to Bitcoin, blockchain, and their broader implications. By the time you finish, you'll not only understand the concepts but also feel confident navigating the fast-evolving landscape of cryptocurrencies and decentralized technology. Here's an overview of what we'll cover:

1. The Origin of Bitcoin: Learn about the history of Bitcoin, the ideas that inspired it, and how it became the first successful cryptocurrency.

2. Understanding Blockchain Technology: Explore the mechanics of blockchain, including how transactions are verified, blocks are created, and consensus is achieved.

3. Other Cryptocurrencies and Use Cases: Discover the world beyond Bitcoin, including Ethereum, smart contracts, and decentralized applications (dApps).

4. Investing and Trading: Gain insights into buying, storing, and trading cryptocurrencies while understanding the risks involved.

5. The Broader Impact of Blockchain: Examine how blockchain is transforming industries and reshaping our digital and economic future.

6. Challenges and Controversies: Delve into the debates surrounding regulation, environmental concerns, and the role of cryptocurrency in illicit activities.

Dispelling Common Myths

Before diving into the details, let's address some common misconceptions about Bitcoin and blockchain:

Myth 1: Bitcoin Is Just a Fad: While some critics dismiss Bitcoin as a speculative bubble, its longevity and growing adoption suggest otherwise. Bitcoin has endured over a decade of scrutiny, proving its resilience and value as a digital asset.

Myth 2: Blockchain Equals Bitcoin: Blockchain is the technology behind Bitcoin, but its applications extend far beyond cryptocurrencies. From tracking supply chains to securing medical records, blockchain is a versatile tool.

Myth 3: Cryptocurrencies Are Only for Tech-Savvy Individuals: While early adopters were often tech enthusiasts, user-friendly wallets, exchanges, and educational resources have made cryptocurrencies more accessible to everyday users.

The Journey Ahead

As you embark on this journey, keep in mind that the world of Bitcoin and blockchain is dynamic and ever-changing. New technologies, regulations, and use cases are constantly emerging, and staying informed is essential. However, at its core, understanding Bitcoin and blockchain boils down to grasping a few key principles: decentralization, transparency, and trustlessness.

Bitcoin and blockchain represent a shift in how we think about money, data, and technology. This shift is not without its challenges, but the potential rewards are immense. Imagine a world where financial systems are more inclusive, supply chains are more transparent, and digital identities are more secure. This is the promise of

Bitcoin and blockchain—a promise we're just beginning to explore.

A Personal Note

I remember the first time I heard about Bitcoin. Like many of you, I was skeptical. The concept of a purely digital currency seemed abstract, even far-fetched. But the more I learned, the more I realized that Bitcoin wasn't just a new form of money—it was a profound innovation with the potential to reshape the world.

This book is my attempt to share that sense of discovery with you. My goal is to break down complex concepts into simple, digestible explanations, so you can see the possibilities for yourself. Whether you're here to explore a new investment opportunity, deepen your technical knowledge, or simply satisfy your curiosity, I'm excited to have you along for the ride.

Ready to Begin?

The journey into Bitcoin and blockchain may seem daunting at first, but don't worry—you don't need to be a programmer or economist to understand it. This book is designed to guide you step by step, starting with the basics and gradually building to more advanced topics.

So, grab a cup of coffee, settle in, and let's dive into the fascinating world of Bitcoin and blockchain. By the end of this book, you'll not only understand these revolutionary technologies but also feel empowered to participate in shaping the future they're creating.

Welcome to the world of decentralized technology—let's get started!

PART 1: Introduction to Cryptocurrencies and Blockchain Technology

1.1. What Are Cryptocurrencies?

Cryptocurrencies are digital or virtual forms of money that use cryptography for security. Unlike traditional currencies issued by governments and central banks, cryptocurrencies operate on decentralized networks based on blockchain technology. The most well-known cryptocurrency, Bitcoin, was introduced in 2009 by an individual or group under the pseudonym Satoshi Nakamoto. Since then, thousands of cryptocurrencies have emerged, each offering unique features and applications.

At their core, cryptocurrencies aim to revolutionize how people exchange value by offering secure, transparent, and efficient methods for transferring wealth. To understand why cryptocurrencies are significant, we must first delve into the evolution of money and the problems cryptocurrencies aim to solve.

1.2. The Evolution of Money

The concept of money has evolved over millennia, from barter systems to the digital payment systems we use today. Understanding this journey helps contextualize the emergence of cryptocurrencies as a natural progression in the history of money.

The Barter System

Before the invention of money, societies relied on barter, exchanging goods and services directly. For instance, a farmer might trade grain for a carpenter's labor. While this system worked in small, localized settings, it had significant limitations:

1. Double Coincidence of Wants: Both parties needed to want what the other offered.

2. Lack of Standard Value: There was no universal measure of value, making trades inconsistent.

3. Indivisibility: Large items like livestock were hard to divide for smaller trades.

These inefficiencies led to the development of money as a medium of exchange.

The Advent of Commodity Money

To overcome the limitations of barter, early civilizations began using commodity money—items with intrinsic value that were widely accepted. Examples include:

Shells: Used by various indigenous cultures.

Salt: Highly valued in ancient Rome and Africa.

Precious Metals: Gold and silver became universal symbols of wealth due to their scarcity and durability.

Commodity money introduced a standardized way to trade but still presented challenges, such as the difficulty of transport and storage.

The Rise of Coinage and Paper Money

Around 600 BCE, the first standardized coins were minted in the ancient kingdom of Lydia (modern-day Turkey). Coins made trade more practical by offering a uniform weight and value.

By the Tang Dynasty in China (618–907 CE), paper money emerged as a solution to the inconvenience of carrying heavy coins. This concept spread to Europe, eventually leading to the issuance of banknotes backed by precious metals.

Fiat Money

In the 20th century, most nations abandoned the gold standard, transitioning to fiat money—currency backed not by a physical commodity but by government decree. Fiat money derives value from trust in the issuing authority. While flexible and scalable, fiat systems are vulnerable to inflation, mismanagement, and political instability.

The Digital Age

The rise of the internet brought digital money into the spotlight. Systems like PayPal and credit cards allowed seamless online transactions. However, these systems still relied on centralized authorities like banks to mediate transactions, often incurring fees and delays.

This dependency on intermediaries paved the way for cryptocurrencies, offering a decentralized alternative to traditional financial systems.

1.3. Why Cryptocurrencies Matter

Cryptocurrencies represent a transformative shift in the way we think about money, ownership, and trust. Their significance lies in addressing the shortcomings of traditional financial systems while introducing innovative possibilities.

1.3.1. Decentralization

Unlike fiat currencies managed by central banks, cryptocurrencies operate on decentralized networks. These networks rely on blockchain technology, a distributed ledger system where transactions are verified by a network of computers (nodes) rather than a single authority.

This decentralization eliminates intermediaries, reducing transaction costs and increasing resilience against corruption, censorship, and systemic failures.

1.3.2. Financial Inclusion

Traditional banking systems often exclude billions of people due to lack of infrastructure, high fees, or stringent identification requirements. Cryptocurrencies offer an alternative for the unbanked population, enabling them to participate in the global economy with just an internet connection and a smartphone.

1.3.3. Transparency and Security

Cryptocurrencies are built on blockchain technology, which provides a transparent and immutable record of all transactions. Key benefits include:

Tamper-Proof Transactions: Once recorded, transactions cannot be altered without network consensus.

Enhanced Privacy: While public blockchains are transparent, user identities are pseudonymous, providing a balance between transparency and privacy.

1.3.4. Low Transaction Costs and Speed

Traditional international payments can take days and incur high fees due to intermediaries. Cryptocurrencies enable near-instantaneous cross-border transactions at a fraction of the cost.

For example, sending Bitcoin from one country to another is as simple as transferring data, with no reliance on banking hours or geographic boundaries.

1.3.5. Hedge Against Inflation

Many cryptocurrencies, like Bitcoin, have a capped supply, meaning no more than a fixed number of coins will ever be created. This contrasts with fiat currencies, which governments can print at will, leading to inflation.

In countries with unstable economies, cryptocurrencies often serve as a store of value, protecting individuals from hyperinflation and currency devaluation.

1.3.6. Programmable Money

Cryptocurrencies like Ethereum introduce the concept of programmable money through smart contracts—self-executing contracts with predefined rules. This innovation enables complex financial operations, such as:

Decentralized Finance (DeFi): Financial services like lending, borrowing, and trading without intermediaries.

Tokenization of Assets: Representing real-world assets like real estate or art as digital tokens on a blockchain.

1.3.7. Empowerment Through Ownership

With cryptocurrencies, individuals gain full control of their funds without relying on banks. This is achieved through cryptographic wallets, which store private keys granting access to one's assets.

However, this also comes with risks: losing private keys means losing access to funds, emphasizing the importance of secure storage.

1.3.8. Potential for Global Impact

Cryptocurrencies have far-reaching implications across industries, including:

Remittances: Reducing fees for migrant workers sending money home.

Charity: Ensuring transparency in donations.

Supply Chain: Enhancing traceability and accountability.

Gaming and Virtual Worlds: Enabling economies within digital ecosystems.

Challenges and Criticisms

Despite their potential, cryptocurrencies face significant challenges:

1. Volatility: Prices can fluctuate dramatically, making them unreliable for everyday use.

2. Regulatory Uncertainty: Governments worldwide grapple with how to regulate cryptocurrencies, balancing innovation with concerns about fraud and illegal activities.

3. Energy Consumption: Some cryptocurrencies, like Bitcoin, require substantial energy for mining, raising environmental concerns. Addressing these challenges is critical for widespread adoption.

Cryptocurrencies mark a pivotal moment in the evolution of money, addressing many of the inefficiencies of traditional financial systems. By offering decentralization, transparency, and financial inclusion, they empower individuals while challenging the status quo.

As the world increasingly embraces digital solutions, understanding cryptocurrencies is essential for navigating the future of finance. In the next chapter, we will explore blockchain technology, the revolutionary system underpinning cryptocurrencies, and its transformative potential across industries.

2. What is Blockchain?

Blockchain is a revolutionary digital technology that acts as a distributed ledger to securely and transparently record transactions and data. It is the underlying foundation for cryptocurrencies like Bitcoin but has applications far beyond digital currencies. Blockchain operates without the need for a central authority, making it decentralized. It is designed to ensure data integrity, immutability, and accessibility across a network of participants.

At its core, a blockchain is a chain of blocks, where each block contains a list of transactions, a timestamp, and a reference to the previous block. These blocks are linked together cryptographically, forming an unbreakable chain of records. Because of its unique properties, blockchain has become a transformative technology, influencing industries such as finance, healthcare, supply chain management, and more.

2.1. How Blockchain Works

Blockchain operates as a decentralized network of nodes (computers) that collectively maintain and update the ledger. Here's a breakdown of how blockchain works:

2.1.1. Creation of a Transaction

When a user initiates a transaction, such as transferring cryptocurrency or recording data, the transaction is broadcast to the blockchain network.

2.1.2. Verification

Before a transaction can be added to the blockchain, it must be verified by network participants (nodes). These nodes use consensus mechanisms such as Proof of Work (PoW) or Proof of Stake (PoS) to validate the transaction's legitimacy.

2.1.3. Grouping into Blocks

Once verified, transactions are grouped together into a block. The block contains several key elements:

- The list of verified transactions
- A timestamp marking when the block was created
- A cryptographic hash of the previous block, which ensures that the blocks are linked

2.1.4. Consensus Mechanism

To ensure the network agrees on the state of the ledger, blockchain employs consensus mechanisms. For example:

- **Proof of Work (PoW):** Miners solve complex mathematical problems to validate and add blocks to the blockchain. This process requires significant computational power.

- **Proof of Stake (PoS):** Validators are chosen to create new blocks based on the amount of cryptocurrency they hold and are willing to "stake" as collateral.

2.1.5. Adding the Block to the Chain

After achieving consensus, the new block is added to the blockchain. Each block is linked to the previous block through its cryptographic hash, creating a secure chain of data.

2.1.6. Immutability

Once a block is added to the blockchain, its contents cannot be altered without modifying all subsequent blocks, which is computationally infeasible. This immutability ensures the integrity and security of the data.

2.1.7. Decentralized Storage

The blockchain is stored across all nodes in the network, ensuring that no single entity has control over the entire system. This decentralization prevents data tampering and improves resilience.

2.2. Key Features of Blockchain Technology

Blockchain technology is distinguished by several key features that make it a robust and innovative solution for digital record-keeping.

2.2.1. Decentralization

Unlike traditional systems that rely on a central authority, blockchain operates on a decentralized network. This eliminates the need for intermediaries, reduces single points of failure, and empowers users to have greater control over their data and transactions.

2.2.2. Transparency

All transactions recorded on a blockchain are visible to all participants in the network. While the identities of users may remain pseudonymous, the transaction data is publicly accessible, fostering trust and accountability.

2.2.3. Immutability

Data recorded on the blockchain cannot be changed or deleted without altering subsequent blocks. This feature ensures the integrity and permanence of the data, making it an ideal solution for auditing and record-keeping.

2.2.4. Security

Blockchain uses advanced cryptographic techniques to secure data. The combination of hashing, encryption, and consensus mechanisms makes it extremely difficult for malicious actors to manipulate the system.

2.2.5. Efficiency

Blockchain can streamline processes by eliminating intermediaries, reducing transaction costs, and speeding up data verification. For example, cross-border payments on a blockchain network are significantly faster than traditional banking systems.

2.2.6. Smart Contracts

Blockchain platforms like Ethereum enable the use of smart contracts—self-executing agreements with predefined conditions. Smart contracts automate processes, reduce human error, and enhance efficiency.

2.2.7. Distributed Ledger

The blockchain's ledger is distributed across all nodes in the network, ensuring redundancy and resilience. This feature makes the system more secure and less prone to downtime.

2.3. Decentralization and Its Benefits

Decentralization is one of the most defining aspects of blockchain technology. It refers to the absence of a central authority or controlling entity. Instead, power and decision-making are distributed across all participants in the network.

2.3.1. What is Decentralization?

In traditional systems, a central authority (like a bank or government) oversees and manages operations. In a decentralized blockchain network, no single entity has control. Instead, all participants work together to maintain and update the ledger.

2.3.2. Benefits of Decentralization

a. Enhanced Security

Decentralization reduces the risk of cyberattacks and data breaches. Since the data is stored across multiple nodes, an attacker would need to compromise the majority of the network to alter the blockchain, which is practically impossible.

b. Greater Transparency

In a decentralized network, all participants have access to the same data, ensuring complete transparency. This is particularly valuable in industries like supply chain management, where stakeholders need to track goods and transactions.

c. Elimination of Intermediaries

By removing intermediaries, blockchain reduces transaction costs and speeds up processes. For instance, in financial services, peer-to-peer transactions on a blockchain eliminate the need for banks or payment processors.

d. Increased Resilience

Decentralized systems are more resilient to failures and outages. Even if some nodes go offline, the blockchain remains operational due to its distributed nature.

e. Empowerment of Individuals

Decentralization gives individuals greater control over their assets and data. For example, with cryptocurrencies, users can manage their funds without relying on banks.

f. Fostering Innovation

Decentralized platforms encourage innovation by providing open-access systems for developers. For instance, blockchain platforms like Ethereum allow developers to create decentralized applications (DApps) and smart contracts.

g. Enhanced Trust

Decentralization builds trust among participants by providing a transparent and tamper-proof system. It ensures that all parties have equal access to data, reducing the need for blind trust in intermediaries.

2.3.3. Challenges of Decentralization

While decentralization offers numerous benefits, it also comes with challenges:

Scalability: Decentralized networks can struggle with high transaction volumes, leading to delays and increased costs.

Complexity: Setting up and maintaining a decentralized network can be technically challenging.

Governance: Decision-making in decentralized systems can be slow and contentious due to the involvement of multiple stakeholders.

Blockchain technology, powered by its decentralized nature, offers unparalleled security, transparency, and efficiency. Its unique features have the potential to transform industries and empower individuals, making it one of the most innovative technologies of our time.

3. The Birth of Bitcoin

The story of Bitcoin's creation is one of innovation, mystery, and revolution. Emerging from the ruins of the 2008 global financial crisis, Bitcoin marked a turning point in the history of finance and technology. This chapter explores the enigmatic figure behind its invention, Satoshi Nakamoto, and the significance of Bitcoin's beginnings, including the Genesis Block.

3.1. The Story of Satoshi Nakamoto

The origin of Bitcoin is inextricably linked to the pseudonymous figure known as Satoshi Nakamoto. Despite years of speculation, Satoshi's true identity remains one of the greatest mysteries in the tech world. Who was Satoshi Nakamoto? Was it an individual, a group of people, or perhaps even a government entity? To this day, the question remains unanswered, and Satoshi's anonymity has only added to the mystique surrounding Bitcoin.

Satoshi's First Appearance

Satoshi Nakamoto first appeared in 2008 with the publication of a white paper titled Bitcoin: A Peer-to-Peer Electronic Cash System. Distributed on a cryptography mailing list, this document outlined a groundbreaking system that combined cryptography, decentralized networks, and game theory to create a form of digital money free from central authorities. The timing of the paper's release was significant: the world was reeling from the collapse of major financial institutions and the global economic downturn. Trust in traditional financial systems was at an all-time low, creating fertile ground for Satoshi's vision.

The Philosophy Behind Bitcoin

Satoshi's writings and code reveal a deep understanding of both computer science and economics. They articulated the flaws in centralized banking, such as inflation, censorship, and reliance on trust in intermediaries. Bitcoin was designed as a solution to these issues, offering a decentralized, transparent, and tamper-resistant alternative.

In their forum posts, Satoshi emphasized Bitcoin's potential to empower individuals by granting them full control over their money. They believed in the principles of financial sovereignty and the democratization of money—a stark contrast to the hierarchical, opaque structures of traditional finance.

The Disappearance of Satoshi

After laying the groundwork for Bitcoin and collaborating with early developers, Satoshi Nakamoto vanished from the public eye in late 2010. Their final known communication was an email stating they had "moved on to other things." Before disappearing, Satoshi transferred control of the Bitcoin repository and alert keys to trusted members of the community, ensuring that Bitcoin would continue to evolve without their direct involvement.

Satoshi's disappearance has sparked endless theories. Some speculate that they feared government persecution, while others believe the mystery was intentional, designed to decentralize Bitcoin's leadership. Whatever the reason, Satoshi's absence has ensured that Bitcoin remains a truly decentralized project, with no single person or entity in control.

3.2. The Genesis Block and Bitcoin's Origins

The technical and philosophical foundation of Bitcoin can be traced back to its first block, known as the Genesis Block. This block, mined by Satoshi Nakamoto on January 3, 2009, is a cornerstone in the history of cryptocurrencies.

The Significance of the Genesis Block

The Genesis Block, or Block 0, was the very first block in Bitcoin's blockchain. It holds a special place in Bitcoin's history, not only because it marked the birth of the network but also because it encapsulated Satoshi's vision. The Genesis Block was hardcoded into Bitcoin's source code and cannot be spent or altered, symbolizing its foundational nature.

What sets the Genesis Block apart is the message embedded within it:

"The Times 03/Jan/2009 Chancellor on brink of second bailout for banks."

This quote, taken from the front page of The Times newspaper on the day the block was mined, serves as a timestamp and a powerful critique of the existing financial system. It highlights the economic context in which Bitcoin was born—a time of widespread dissatisfaction with banks, government bailouts, and financial inequality.

Technical Details of the Genesis Block

The Genesis Block contains a reward of 50 bitcoins, but unlike subsequent blocks, these coins cannot be spent due to how the block was constructed. This limitation adds to the block's symbolic nature, making it a monument rather than a functional transaction. The block hash, a unique identifier, is another aspect of its uniqueness, as it does not conform to the usual difficulty rules of Bitcoin's proof-of-work algorithm.

In technical terms, the Genesis Block laid the groundwork for Bitcoin's decentralized ledger. Its creation established key concepts such as:

Blockchain Architecture: The Genesis Block was the first link in what would become a continuous, immutable chain of data blocks.

Mining Rewards: By including a reward of 50 bitcoins, it demonstrated the incentive structure that would drive miners to maintain the network.

Proof-of-Work: The block illustrated the consensus mechanism that ensures the integrity and security of Bitcoin's decentralized system.

The Early Network

Following the creation of the Genesis Block, Satoshi Nakamoto mined the next several blocks to build out the network. During these early stages, Bitcoin had no monetary value and was primarily a proof of concept. The small community of cryptography enthusiasts who participated did so out of curiosity and a shared belief in the potential of decentralized money.

The first transaction on the Bitcoin network occurred when Satoshi sent 10 bitcoins to Hal Finney, a renowned cryptographer and early Bitcoin supporter. This transaction, recorded in Block 170, demonstrated Bitcoin's practical functionality as a peer-to-peer payment system.

Bitcoin's First Steps Towards Adoption

In its infancy, Bitcoin remained a niche experiment, discussed mainly on cryptography forums. However, the seeds of its revolutionary potential had been planted. Early adopters, such as Hal Finney, Nick Szabo, and others, recognized the profound implications of Bitcoin's design and began contributing to its development.

One of the first major milestones in Bitcoin's journey toward mainstream recognition was the infamous

"Bitcoin Pizza Day" in May 2010. A programmer named Laszlo Hanyecz used 10,000 bitcoins to purchase two pizzas, marking the first real-world transaction with Bitcoin. At the time, this transaction seemed trivial, but it symbolized Bitcoin's evolution from an abstract concept to a functional currency.

The birth of Bitcoin is a story of ingenuity and rebellion. It represents a bold response to the failings of traditional finance, offering a new vision of money and economic freedom. Satoshi Nakamoto's invention, embodied in the Genesis Block, set the stage for a decentralized financial revolution that continues to unfold. As we delve deeper into Bitcoin's history and mechanics, we gain a greater appreciation for the groundbreaking ideas that brought it to life.

PART 2: Understanding Bitcoin

4. How Bitcoin Works

Bitcoin is often described as a revolutionary digital currency, but what truly sets it apart is the underlying technology and mechanisms that power it. In this chapter, we will explore the core workings of Bitcoin, focusing on transactions, mining, and the role of nodes. These elements form the foundation of the Bitcoin network, ensuring its functionality, security, and decentralization.

4.1. Bitcoin Transactions Explained

At the heart of the Bitcoin network lies the transaction system, which allows users to send and receive funds digitally without a central authority. Bitcoin transactions consist of three main components: inputs, outputs, and a digital signature.

Inputs and Outputs

A Bitcoin transaction essentially takes inputs (the source of the funds) and assigns them to outputs (the recipient). The inputs are references to previous transactions, proving the sender has the Bitcoin they claim to own. Outputs indicate the new owner(s) of the transferred Bitcoin.

For example, imagine Alice wants to send 0.5 Bitcoin to Bob. She uses an input linked to a prior transaction where she received 1 Bitcoin. The transaction output directs 0.5 Bitcoin to Bob's Bitcoin address and returns the remaining 0.5 Bitcoin as "change" back to Alice.

Public and Private Keys

Each Bitcoin user has a pair of cryptographic keys:

Public Key: Acts as the user's Bitcoin address where funds can be sent.

Private Key: A secret key used to sign transactions, proving ownership and authorization.

When Alice sends Bitcoin to Bob, her private key generates a digital signature, ensuring the transaction's authenticity. Without the private key, no one can authorize the spending of Bitcoin.

Transaction Validation

Before a transaction is finalized, it must be validated by nodes on the network. Nodes verify:

1. The sender has sufficient funds.
2. The digital signature is valid.
3. The transaction adheres to the network's rules.

Once verified, the transaction enters a pool of unconfirmed transactions called the mempool and awaits inclusion in a block through the mining process.

Fees and Prioritization

Bitcoin transactions often include a fee paid to miners. This fee incentivizes miners to prioritize certain transactions over others. Higher fees result in faster confirmations, making them crucial during periods of high network congestion.

4.2. Mining and the Creation of New Bitcoins

Bitcoin mining serves two critical purposes:

1. Validating and securing transactions.
2. Creating new bitcoins in a controlled manner.

What is Bitcoin Mining?

Bitcoin mining is the process of solving complex mathematical problems to add new blocks to the blockchain. This is done using specialized hardware, known as mining rigs. Miners compete to solve a cryptographic puzzle, and the first to succeed earns the right to add a block of transactions to the blockchain.

Proof of Work (PoW)

The Bitcoin network relies on a consensus mechanism called Proof of Work. Here's how it works:

1. Miners solve a computational problem by finding a specific hash value (a string of characters).
2. The solution must meet the network's difficulty target, which adjusts every 2016 blocks (roughly every two weeks) to maintain a block creation time of about 10 minutes.

This process ensures fairness and prevents any single entity from dominating the network.

Block Rewards

When a miner successfully mines a block, they receive a block reward composed of:

1. Newly Minted Bitcoins: These are created as part of the mining process. The reward started at 50 BTC in 2009 and is halved approximately every four years in an event called the halving. As of 2024, the reward stands at 6.25 BTC per block.

2. Transaction Fees: Collected from the transactions included in the block.

Over time, block rewards will diminish, and miners will rely entirely on transaction fees for compensation.

Environmental Concerns

Bitcoin mining requires significant computational power, consuming large amounts of electricity. This has raised concerns about its environmental impact, especially in regions where electricity is generated from non-renewable sources. Efforts are ongoing to shift mining operations to renewable energy sources.

4.3. The Role of Nodes in the Bitcoin Network

Nodes are a crucial component of Bitcoin's decentralized architecture. They are devices, such as computers or servers, that run the Bitcoin software, maintaining the network's integrity and security.

Types of Nodes

1. Full Nodes:

Full nodes store a complete copy of the blockchain, validating and relaying transactions and blocks. They are vital for ensuring the network's accuracy and trustworthiness. Full nodes enforce Bitcoin's rules, rejecting invalid transactions or blocks.

2. Light Nodes:

Also known as lightweight clients, these nodes do not store the entire blockchain. Instead, they rely on full nodes to retrieve transaction and block data. Light nodes are more resource-efficient, making them suitable for mobile and low-power devices.

3. Mining Nodes:

These nodes are operated by miners and include the additional functionality required to participate in the mining process. Mining nodes validate transactions and compete to create new blocks.

Node Functions

- **Transaction Validation:** Nodes check that transactions meet the protocol's rules.

- **Block Verification:** Nodes verify the legitimacy of new blocks added to the blockchain.

- **Relaying Data:** Nodes share transaction and block data with other nodes, ensuring the network remains synchronized.

- **Enforcing Consensus Rules:** Nodes enforce Bitcoin's core rules, such as the 21 million Bitcoin supply limit and the difficulty adjustment mechanism.

Decentralization Through Nodes

The distributed nature of nodes is what makes Bitcoin resistant to censorship and tampering. No single entity controls the network, as thousands of nodes worldwide collectively maintain the blockchain.

Running a Node

Anyone can run a Bitcoin node by downloading the Bitcoin Core software. While it requires storage and bandwidth, running a node strengthens the network and contributes to its decentralization. Node operators do not earn financial rewards but gain increased privacy and direct participation in the Bitcoin ecosystem.

Bitcoin operates through a seamless interplay of transactions, mining, and nodes. Transactions represent the exchange of value, mining ensures security and adds new bitcoins to circulation, and nodes maintain the network's decentralized structure. Together, these elements create a trustless and transparent system, empowering users to transact freely without intermediaries. By understanding these foundational components, you can grasp how Bitcoin continues to function as a revolutionary form of digital currency.

5. Buying, Selling, and Using Bitcoin

Bitcoin has evolved from being an obscure digital currency to a mainstream financial instrument. In this chapter, we explore the practical steps to get started with Bitcoin, from setting up a wallet to trading on exchanges, and finally, how Bitcoin is being used in the real world. Whether you are a complete novice or a curious investor, this guide will equip you with the tools to navigate Bitcoin's ecosystem confidently.

5.1. Setting Up a Bitcoin Wallet

A Bitcoin wallet is a digital tool that allows you to store, receive, and send Bitcoin. It functions like a bank account for your cryptocurrency, providing both security and accessibility.

Here's a step-by-step guide to setting up your Bitcoin wallet:

1. Choosing the Right Type of Wallet

Bitcoin wallets come in several types, each offering distinct advantages and trade-offs:

- **Hot Wallets:** Connected to the internet, these are easy to use but more vulnerable to hacking. Examples include mobile wallets like Trust Wallet and desktop wallets like Electrum.
- **Cold Wallets:** Offline wallets, such as hardware wallets (Ledger, Trezor) or paper wallets, are highly secure and ideal for long-term storage.
- **Custodial Wallets:** Provided by exchanges, these wallets are convenient for frequent traders but give control of your private keys to the platform.

2. Downloading and Installing a Wallet

Once you've selected a wallet type, follow these steps:

- Visit the official website or app store of your chosen wallet provider.
- Download and install the application on your device.
- Complete the setup process by following the on-screen instructions.

3. Backing Up Your Wallet

Security is paramount. Wallets generate a recovery phrase or private key during setup.

Recovery Phrase: Write down the 12–24 words in order and store them securely offline.

Private Key: Keep it confidential; anyone with access can control your funds.

4. Funding Your Wallet

After setting up, you can fund your wallet by purchasing Bitcoin on an exchange or receiving Bitcoin from another user. Use your wallet's public address to receive payments.

5.2. Exchanges: Buying and Selling Bitcoin

Bitcoin exchanges act as marketplaces where buyers and sellers trade Bitcoin and other cryptocurrencies. Understanding how to use exchanges is essential for acquiring or cashing out Bitcoin.

1. Choosing a Reputable Exchange

When selecting an exchange, consider these factors:

- **Security:** Look for exchanges with two-factor authentication (2FA) and insurance coverage for funds (e.g., Coinbase, Binance).

- **Fees:** Review trading, deposit, and withdrawal fees.

- **Regulation:** Opt for exchanges that comply with local laws and have a transparent reputation.

2. Creating an Account

To start trading, follow these steps:

- Sign up on the exchange's platform using your email or phone number.
- Complete the identity verification (KYC) process, which usually involves uploading identification documents.

3. Buying Bitcoin

Once your account is set up:

- Deposit fiat currency (e.g., USD, EUR) using bank transfer, credit card, or other supported payment methods.
- Place a buy order by specifying the amount of Bitcoin or fiat currency you want to spend.

4. Selling Bitcoin

Selling Bitcoin is the reverse process:

- Transfer Bitcoin to your exchange wallet.
- Place a sell order, choosing between market price (instant sale) or limit price (selling at a specific value).

5. Safeguarding Your Assets

After purchasing Bitcoin, it's wise to transfer it to a private wallet, especially if you're not planning to trade actively. Leaving funds on exchanges exposes you to hacking risks.

5.3. Real-World Applications of Bitcoin

Bitcoin's utility has grown significantly since its inception. While initially perceived as an experimental currency, Bitcoin is now used in various real-world applications.

1. Online Payments

Many online merchants and service providers accept Bitcoin as payment, enabling users to buy goods, services, or subscriptions. Platforms like Overstock, Shopify, and even Microsoft allow Bitcoin transactions.

2. Remittances

Bitcoin simplifies international money transfers by eliminating intermediaries like banks, reducing fees and transaction times. It is particularly useful for sending remittances to countries with limited banking infrastructure.

3. Investment and Savings

Bitcoin is often referred to as "digital gold" because of its potential to act as a store of value.

- **Holding:** Investors buy and hold Bitcoin long-term, betting on its appreciation.
- **Diversification:** Bitcoin is increasingly included in investment portfolios to hedge against inflation and economic uncertainty.

4. Charitable Donations

Organizations such as the Red Cross and Save the Children accept Bitcoin donations. Cryptocurrency donations provide transparency in fund allocation, as transactions can be traced on the blockchain.

5. Decentralized Finance (DeFi)

Although Ethereum dominates the DeFi space, Bitcoin plays a role through tokenized forms like Wrapped Bitcoin (WBTC). These assets allow users to earn interest, provide liquidity, or trade in DeFi ecosystems.

6. Microtransactions and Tips

Bitcoin enables small payments without the high fees associated with traditional payment systems. Content creators on platforms like Twitter or Reddit receive tips in Bitcoin from supporters worldwide.

7. Gaming and Virtual Goods

Bitcoin is gaining traction in online gaming, where players use it to purchase in-game items, trade virtual goods, or even win Bitcoin as rewards.

8. Real Estate

Bitcoin has entered the property market, with some real estate agents accepting it as payment for houses or apartments. These transactions are streamlined through blockchain-based contracts.

9. Cross-Border Trade

Businesses engaged in international trade use Bitcoin to bypass currency conversion fees and delays associated with traditional banking systems.

10. Future Applications

Innovations like the Lightning Network aim to make Bitcoin faster and more scalable, unlocking new possibilities such as streaming payments, smart contracts, and integration with the Internet of Things (IoT).

Buying, selling, and using Bitcoin involves more than just financial transactions—it represents participation in a global movement toward decentralized technology. By setting up a secure wallet, leveraging trusted exchanges, and exploring Bitcoin's diverse applications, you can become an active participant in this transformative digital revolution.

This chapter equips you with the foundational skills to navigate Bitcoin, but it is only the beginning. As you delve deeper, you will discover the profound impact Bitcoin has on finance, commerce, and technology.

6. Bitcoin Security and Privacy

As cryptocurrencies gain popularity, security and privacy remain at the forefront of concerns for both new and seasoned users. While Bitcoin offers a revolutionary way to transact and store value, it also introduces new risks that require a solid understanding of how to protect your assets and safeguard your privacy. In this chapter, we will explore how to secure your Bitcoin wallet, recognize and avoid common scams, and understand the role of anonymity in Bitcoin transactions.

6.1. Protecting Your Wallet

Your Bitcoin wallet is essentially your gateway to the cryptocurrency world. It holds the private keys required to access and manage your Bitcoin. Protecting this wallet is critical, as losing your private keys means losing access to your funds forever.

Types of Wallets and Their Security Features

1. Hardware Wallets:

- Hardware wallets, like Ledger and Trezor, are physical devices that store your private keys offline.

- They are immune to online hacking attempts, making them one of the most secure options.
- To use them, you connect the device to your computer or mobile phone and confirm transactions physically.

2. Software Wallets:

- These include desktop, mobile, and web wallets.
- While convenient, they are more vulnerable to hacking and malware attacks.
- Examples include Exodus, Mycelium, and Electrum.

3. Paper Wallets:

- A paper wallet involves printing your private and public keys on paper and storing it securely.
- Though secure from online threats, they can be easily damaged or lost.

4. Custodial Wallets:
- Custodial wallets, like those offered by exchanges (e.g., Coinbase or Binance), manage your private keys for you.
- While convenient, this approach means trusting a third party with your funds.

Best Practices for Wallet Security

1. Enable Two-Factor Authentication (2FA):

- Always enable 2FA on wallets and exchange accounts to add an extra layer of protection.
- Use authentication apps like Google Authenticator instead of SMS-based 2FA, which is susceptible to SIM-swapping attacks.

2. Use Strong and Unique Passwords:

- A robust password should combine uppercase and lowercase letters, numbers, and symbols.
- Avoid reusing passwords from other accounts.

3. Keep Backup Copies:

- Store your wallet recovery phrase (seed phrase) in multiple secure locations.
- Never share your seed phrase with anyone, as it grants full access to your wallet.

4. Keep Software Updated:

- Ensure your wallet software and firmware are always up to date to benefit from the latest security patches.

5. Avoid Public Wi-Fi:

- Refrain from accessing your wallet using public Wi-Fi networks, which may be insecure.
- If necessary, use a virtual private network (VPN) to encrypt your connection.

6. Cold Storage:

- For long-term holding, consider cold storage solutions like hardware wallets or paper wallets.
- Cold storage keeps your funds offline, reducing the risk of hacks.

6.2. Common Scams and How to Avoid Them

The rapid adoption of Bitcoin has attracted not only enthusiasts but also scammers looking to exploit unsuspecting users. Recognizing common scams is crucial to safeguarding your assets.

Types of Scams

1. Phishing Scams:

- Scammers create fake websites or send emails impersonating trusted entities (e.g., exchanges or wallets).
- Victims are tricked into entering their login credentials or private keys.

2. Ponzi Schemes and Fake Investment Opportunities:

- Promises of guaranteed high returns or "double your Bitcoin" offers are often scams.
- Pyramid schemes also lure users into investing in non-existent projects.

3. Fake Wallet Apps:

- Fraudulent apps posing as legitimate wallets can steal private keys.
- Always download wallet apps from official websites or app stores.

4. Social Engineering:

- Scammers manipulate users into revealing sensitive information through direct messages or phone calls.
- For example, impersonators may claim to be customer support agents.

5. Giveaway Scams:

- Scammers on social media promise to send back double the Bitcoin if users send a specific amount.
- These giveaways are fake and a common tactic used by fraudsters.

6. Ransomware:

- Malware infects a user's device and encrypts their data, demanding Bitcoin payment for restoration.
- Ransomware attacks target individuals and businesses alike.

7. SIM-Swapping Attacks:

- Attackers gain control of your mobile number to bypass SMS-based 2FA and access your accounts.

How to Avoid Scams

1. Verify Websites and Emails:

- Check URLs for accuracy before entering sensitive information.
- Avoid clicking on links in unsolicited emails.

2. Be Skeptical of "Too Good to Be True" Offers:

- Guaranteed returns or pressure to act quickly are red flags.
- Conduct thorough research before investing in any project.

3. Use Official Channels:

- Download wallet software or apps from official sources.
- Verify social media accounts of exchanges or services to avoid imposters.

4. Enable Strong Security Features:

- Use 2FA, strong passwords, and hardware wallets whenever possible.
- Keep backup copies of critical data.

5. Educate Yourself:

- Stay informed about the latest scams and tactics used by fraudsters.
- Join trusted communities and forums to learn from experienced users.

6.3. The Role of Anonymity in Bitcoin

Bitcoin is often associated with anonymity, but it is more accurately described as pseudonymous. While your real identity is not directly tied to your Bitcoin address, transactions are recorded on a public ledger, making them traceable under certain conditions.

How Bitcoin Provides Pseudonymity

1. Public Keys:

- Transactions are conducted using public addresses (derived from private keys), not personal information.
- Each transaction is recorded on the blockchain, but the identity behind the address remains hidden.

2. Blockchain Transparency:

- Bitcoin's blockchain is publicly accessible, allowing anyone to view transaction histories.
- However, unless a Bitcoin address is linked to a real identity (e.g., through an exchange), the user remains pseudonymous.

3. Privacy-Enhancing Tools:

- Tools like mixers or tumblers break the link between Bitcoin addresses to enhance anonymity.
- Privacy-focused wallets (e.g., Wasabi Wallet) offer additional features to obscure transactions.

Challenges to Bitcoin Anonymity

1. KYC Regulations:

- Many exchanges and services require Know Your Customer (KYC) compliance, tying Bitcoin addresses to real identities.

2. Blockchain Analysis:

- Companies like Chainalysis use sophisticated tools to trace Bitcoin transactions and link them to individuals.

3. Reuse of Addresses:

- Using the same Bitcoin address for multiple transactions can reveal patterns that compromise privacy.

4. IP Address Exposure:

- Transactions broadcast directly from your IP address can potentially link your identity to your Bitcoin activity.

Best Practices for Enhancing Anonymity

1. Use New Addresses for Each Transaction:

- Avoid address reuse to minimize traceability.

2. Use Privacy-Focused Wallets:

- These wallets provide features like CoinJoin, which combines multiple transactions to obscure their origins.

3. Avoid Publicly Sharing Addresses:

- Posting your Bitcoin address on social media or forums can link it to your identity.

4. Use Tor or VPN:

- When accessing the Bitcoin network, use Tor or a VPN to hide your IP address.

5. Consider Privacy Coins:

- For heightened anonymity, consider using privacy-focused cryptocurrencies like Monero or Zcash.

Security and privacy are the foundation of a safe and effective Bitcoin experience. By understanding how to protect your wallet, recognizing and avoiding common scams, and using tools to enhance anonymity, you can navigate the cryptocurrency space with confidence. While Bitcoin offers significant advantages, it also places responsibility on users to safeguard their assets and information. Mastering these skills is essential for anyone looking to embrace the potential of Bitcoin and blockchain technology.

PART 3: Blockchain Beyond Bitcoin

7. Altcoins and Their Ecosystem

The world of cryptocurrency extends far beyond Bitcoin. Altcoins, or "alternative coins," represent a vast and diverse segment of the cryptocurrency market. They aim to address perceived limitations in Bitcoin or offer entirely new functionalities and use cases. This chapter delves into the concept of altcoins, explores key examples like Ethereum and Litecoin, and examines how they differ from Bitcoin.

7.1. What Are Altcoins?

The term "altcoin" refers to all cryptocurrencies other than Bitcoin. These alternatives were developed to build upon, expand, or modify the concepts introduced by Bitcoin. Since the launch of Bitcoin in 2009, thousands of altcoins have been created, each seeking to carve out its niche in the blockchain ecosystem.

Purpose of Altcoins

Altcoins exist for various reasons, including:

1. Improved Functionality: Some altcoins address specific weaknesses in Bitcoin, such as transaction speed, scalability, or energy consumption.

2. New Use Cases: Others aim to expand the blockchain's utility beyond digital currency, enabling applications like smart contracts, decentralized finance (DeFi), or privacy-enhanced transactions.

3. Experimentation: Altcoins often serve as platforms for testing new ideas and technologies in blockchain and cryptocurrency.

Types of Altcoins

1. Mining-Based Altcoins: These rely on proof-of-work (PoW) mechanisms similar to Bitcoin. Litecoin and Monero are prominent examples.

2. Stablecoins: Pegged to stable assets like fiat currency or gold, stablecoins such as Tether (USDT) and USD Coin (USDC) minimize volatility.

3. Utility Tokens: Designed to grant access to a specific product or service within a blockchain ecosystem, such as Chainlink (LINK) or Filecoin (FIL).

4. Governance Tokens: These provide holders with voting rights in decentralized networks. Uniswap (UNI) is an example.

5. Privacy Coins: Cryptocurrencies like Monero and Zcash prioritize transaction anonymity.

Altcoins enrich the cryptocurrency landscape by introducing innovation and diversity, catering to various user needs and preferences.

7.2. Key Altcoins: Ethereum, Litecoin, and More

While thousands of altcoins exist, a few stand out due to their market impact, technological innovation, and broad adoption. Let's explore some of the most influential altcoins.

Ethereum (ETH)

Ethereum is perhaps the most significant altcoin, with a market capitalization second only to Bitcoin. It introduced the concept of a "smart contract" platform, transforming blockchain technology into a tool for building decentralized applications (dApps).

1. Key Features of Ethereum:

Smart Contracts: Self-executing contracts with terms written into code.

Ethereum Virtual Machine (EVM): A decentralized computing platform enabling developers to create and deploy dApps.

Transition to Proof-of-Stake (PoS): Ethereum has shifted from a PoW system to a PoS system with Ethereum 2.0, enhancing scalability and energy efficiency.

2. Use Cases:

- **Decentralized Finance (DeFi):** Platforms like Aave and Uniswap operate on Ethereum.
- **Non-Fungible Tokens (NFTs):** Ethereum is the leading blockchain for NFT transactions, enabling unique digital asset ownership.

Litecoin (LTC)

Created in 2011 by Charlie Lee, Litecoin is one of the oldest altcoins. It was designed as a "lighter" version of Bitcoin, emphasizing speed and lower transaction costs.

1. **Key Features of Litecoin:**

    - **Faster Transactions:** Litecoin's block generation time is 2.5 minutes compared to Bitcoin's 10 minutes.
    - **Scrypt Algorithm:** A less resource-intensive algorithm than Bitcoin's SHA-256, making mining more accessible.
    - **Limited Supply:** Litecoin's maximum supply is capped at 84 million coins, four times that of Bitcoin.

2. **Use Cases:**

    - **Micropayments:** Its lower fees and faster processing make Litecoin ideal for small transactions.
    - **Payment Integration:** Many merchants accept Litecoin due to its efficiency.

Cardano (ADA)

Cardano aims to combine academic research with blockchain technology. Its layered architecture separates the computation of smart contracts from the transaction ledger, improving scalability and security.

1. Key Features:

Proof-of-Stake Protocol: Cardano uses Ouroboros, an energy-efficient PoS mechanism.
Scientific Approach: Cardano's development is guided by peer-reviewed research and formal methods.

2. Use Cases:

- Education and identity management in developing countries.
- Building sustainable and scalable dApps.

Ripple (XRP)

Ripple focuses on enabling fast, low-cost cross-border payments for banks and financial institutions. Unlike Bitcoin, Ripple uses a unique consensus algorithm rather than mining.

1. Key Features:

- **RippleNet:** A network for real-time gross settlements.
- **XRP Ledger:** A public blockchain optimized for payments.

2. Use Cases:

- Facilitating international money transfers.
- Serving as a bridge currency for fiat-to-fiat transactions.

Polkadot (DOT)

Polkadot enables interoperability among blockchains, allowing them to share data and work together seamlessly.

1. Key Features:

- **Relay Chain:** The central chain coordinating transactions between parachains.
- **Parachains:** Customizable blockchains optimized for specific use cases.

2. Use Cases:

- Building interoperable decentralized ecosystems.
- Connecting private and public blockchains.

Other notable altcoins include Binance Coin (BNB), known for powering the Binance ecosystem; Solana (SOL), celebrated for its high-speed transactions; and

Dogecoin (DOGE), initially created as a meme but now widely recognized.

7.3. How Altcoins Differ from Bitcoin

Altcoins often differentiate themselves from Bitcoin by introducing new features, mechanisms, or philosophies. Here are some key distinctions:

1. Technological Differences

Consensus Mechanisms:
- Bitcoin uses proof-of-work (PoW), which is secure but energy-intensive.
- Many altcoins, such as Ethereum 2.0 and Cardano, use proof-of-stake (PoS), which is more energy-efficient.

Transaction Speed and Scalability:
- Bitcoin can process approximately 7 transactions per second (TPS).
- Altcoins like Solana boast speeds of up to 65,000 TPS.

Privacy Enhancements:
- Bitcoin transactions are pseudonymous but traceable. Privacy coins like Monero and Zcash offer untraceable transactions.

2. Purpose and Use Cases

- **Bitcoin:** Primarily a store of value and digital gold.
- **Altcoins:** Serve diverse purposes, such as enabling smart contracts (Ethereum), facilitating cross-border payments (Ripple), or supporting decentralized storage (Filecoin).

3. Development Philosophy

- **Bitcoin:** Conservative and stable, with limited updates to its codebase to maintain reliability.
- **Altcoins:** More experimental, rapidly evolving to test new ideas and applications.

4. Community and Governance

- **Bitcoin:** Development is guided by consensus within the global Bitcoin community.
- **Altcoins:** Many, like Cardano and Polkadot, include formal governance structures, allowing token holders to vote on network upgrades.

5. Market Dynamics

- **Market Share:** Bitcoin dominates the market, holding around 40-50% of total cryptocurrency market capitalization. Altcoins collectively represent the remaining share.
- **Volatility:** Altcoins are generally more volatile than Bitcoin due to lower liquidity and market capitalization.

6. Mining and Energy Consumption

- Bitcoin mining consumes significant energy due to its PoW mechanism.
- Altcoins like Ethereum (post-merge) and Cardano use PoS, significantly reducing their environmental impact.

Altcoins play an essential role in the cryptocurrency ecosystem. They introduce innovations, expand blockchain use cases, and provide alternatives for those seeking more specialized or advanced features than Bitcoin offers. As the ecosystem matures, altcoins will likely continue to grow in prominence, shaping the future of blockchain technology.

8. Smart Contracts and Decentralized Applications (dApps)

The rise of blockchain technology has opened doors to innovations beyond digital currencies like Bitcoin. Two groundbreaking developments that leverage blockchain's capabilities are smart contracts and decentralized applications (dApps). These technologies have the potential to revolutionize industries by automating processes, ensuring transparency, and removing intermediaries. In this chapter, we explore the foundational concepts of smart contracts and dApps, their functioning, and their real-life applications.

8.1. Introduction to Smart Contracts

A smart contract is a self-executing contract with the terms of the agreement between buyer and seller directly written into lines of code. Running on blockchain networks, these contracts automatically enforce and execute the agreed terms without the need for intermediaries, making transactions more efficient and secure.

Characteristics of Smart Contracts

1. Autonomous: Once deployed, smart contracts operate automatically without human intervention.
2. Immutable: The code and terms cannot be altered once uploaded to the blockchain, ensuring trust and transparency.
3. Decentralized: Smart contracts are executed on a blockchain network, ensuring no single entity controls the process.
4. Transparent: All participants can view the terms of the contract, eliminating ambiguity or disputes.

How Smart Contracts Work

Smart contracts follow the "if-then" logic.

For example:
- If a user sends cryptocurrency to a specified wallet address, then the ownership of an asset is transferred automatically.

This execution is possible through blockchain nodes that verify and validate the conditions of the contract.

Advantages of Smart Contracts

1. Efficiency: Automating processes eliminates delays caused by manual interventions.
2. Cost Savings: Cutting out intermediaries reduces transaction costs.
3. Accuracy: The code enforces terms without human error or misinterpretation.
4. Security: Blockchain encryption makes smart contracts tamper-proof.

Limitations of Smart Contracts

1. Complexity: Designing and coding error-free smart contracts require expertise.
2. Rigidity: Once deployed, contracts cannot be changed, even if errors exist.
3. Legal Ambiguity: Smart contracts are still in a legal gray area in many jurisdictions.

Popular Blockchains for Smart Contracts

Ethereum: The pioneer and most widely used platform for smart contracts.
Binance Smart Chain (BSC): Known for low transaction fees and fast execution.
Solana: Offers high throughput and scalability for smart contract execution.

Cardano: Focuses on security and formal verification of smart contracts.

Examples of Smart Contracts in Action

1. **Real Estate:** Automating property sales by transferring ownership upon payment.
2. **Supply Chain:** Tracking goods and releasing payments when delivery conditions are met.
3. **Insurance:** Triggering payouts automatically based on verifiable events like flight delays.

8.2. Real-Life Use Cases of dApps

Decentralized applications (dApps) are applications that run on a blockchain network rather than centralized servers. These apps leverage the power of smart contracts to provide decentralized, secure, and transparent services. Unlike traditional apps, dApps eliminate single points of failure, making them resilient and censorship-resistant.

Characteristics of dApps

1. **Open Source:** dApps often have publicly available code, enabling trust and collaboration.

2. Decentralized Data: User data is stored on a blockchain or distributed network rather than a centralized database.

3. Tokenized Ecosystem: Many dApps use tokens to incentivize users and manage transactions.

Categories of dApps

1. Finance (DeFi): Decentralized finance applications like lending platforms and decentralized exchanges (DEXs).

2. Gaming: Blockchain-based games with play-to-earn models and ownership of in-game assets through NFTs.

3. Social Media: Platforms that reward users with tokens for their content and engagement.

4. Healthcare: Securely managing patient data and enabling transparent medical research.

5. Supply Chain: Tracking and verifying product journeys from origin to consumer.

Real-Life dApp Use Cases

Here are several examples of how dApps are being used to transform industries:

1. Finance and Banking

One of the most significant use cases of dApps is in the Decentralized Finance (DeFi) sector. DeFi dApps enable financial services like lending, borrowing, trading, and investing without traditional intermediaries like banks.

Example: Uniswap, a decentralized exchange, allows users to trade cryptocurrencies directly from their wallets without needing a centralized exchange.
Impact: Lower transaction costs, faster settlements, and greater financial inclusion.

2. Supply Chain Management

Blockchain-based dApps provide end-to-end visibility in supply chains, reducing fraud and improving efficiency.
Example: VeChain tracks goods throughout the supply chain and verifies authenticity, ensuring transparency for consumers and businesses.
Impact: Enhanced trust in product authenticity and reduced losses from counterfeit goods.

3. Gaming and Entertainment

dApps have revolutionized gaming by introducing play-to-earn models and true ownership of digital assets through Non-Fungible Tokens (NFTs).

Example: Axie Infinity, a blockchain-based game, allows players to earn cryptocurrency by playing and trading in-game assets.

Impact: Players can monetize their gaming skills and truly own in-game items.

4. Healthcare

dApps in healthcare ensure secure and decentralized storage of sensitive medical data, making it accessible only to authorized parties.

Example: Medicalchain provides a platform for managing and sharing health records while maintaining patient privacy.

Impact: Reduced administrative costs and improved patient care coordination.

5. Social Media and Content Creation

Decentralized social media platforms give users control over their data and reward content creators with tokens.

Example: Steemit rewards users for posting and curating content with its native cryptocurrency.

Impact: More equitable revenue-sharing models and reduced censorship.

6. Energy Trading

Energy dApps enable peer-to-peer trading of renewable energy without centralized power companies.

Example: Power Ledger allows users to sell excess solar energy directly to others in their community.
Impact: Promotes renewable energy adoption and decentralizes energy markets.

7. Charity and Fundraising

Blockchain dApps ensure transparency in donations, tracking every transaction to ensure funds reach the intended recipients.

Example: Giveth is a platform for transparent and decentralized philanthropy.
Impact: Increased trust in charitable organizations and better donor engagement.

Challenges in dApp Development

1. Scalability: Many blockchains face limitations in handling large transaction volumes.
2. User Adoption: Non-tech-savvy users may find it challenging to interact with dApps.

3. Regulatory Hurdles: Uncertainty around blockchain technology regulations can deter adoption.
4. Development Complexity: Building secure and efficient dApps requires advanced expertise.

The Future of dApps

The ecosystem of dApps is rapidly growing, with significant improvements in scalability, user experience, and interoperability. Emerging technologies like Layer 2 solutions and cross-chain platforms are addressing existing challenges, paving the way for widespread adoption across industries.

Smart contracts and dApps exemplify the transformative potential of blockchain technology. By automating processes and decentralizing applications, these innovations are poised to disrupt traditional systems and drive efficiency, transparency, and inclusivity across sectors. From finance to healthcare, gaming, and beyond, the possibilities are limitless, making smart contracts and dApps essential pillars of the blockchain revolution.

9. The Rise of Decentralized Finance (DeFi)

Decentralized Finance, commonly known as DeFi, represents a revolutionary shift in the financial industry. It utilizes blockchain technology to offer financial services without relying on traditional banks or centralized institutions. DeFi has been lauded for its ability to democratize access to financial systems, providing opportunities for anyone with an internet connection to participate. In this chapter, we'll explore the core aspects of DeFi, its popular platforms and applications, and the associated risks and rewards.

9.1. What is DeFi?

DeFi, short for Decentralized Finance, refers to a financial ecosystem built on blockchain technology that eliminates intermediaries like banks and financial institutions. DeFi relies on smart contracts—self-executing contracts with predefined terms and conditions written in code—to facilitate transactions and automate processes. By leveraging the transparency, security, and decentralization of blockchain, DeFi creates an open and inclusive financial system.

Key Features of DeFi:

1. Permissionless Access: Anyone with a digital wallet and internet connection can access DeFi services without undergoing traditional Know Your Customer (KYC) or credit checks.

2. Transparency: All transactions and operations are recorded on public blockchains, making them verifiable and immutable.

3. Interoperability: DeFi platforms are often built on open-source protocols, enabling seamless integration and interaction between different applications.

4. Automation through Smart Contracts: Smart contracts replace traditional intermediaries, ensuring efficiency and reducing the potential for human error or fraud.

Core Components of DeFi:

- **Lending and Borrowing:** DeFi platforms like Aave and Compound allow users to lend their assets for interest or borrow against their crypto holdings as collateral.

- **Decentralized Exchanges (DEXs):** Platforms such as Uniswap and SushiSwap enable peer-to-peer trading of cryptocurrencies without relying on centralized exchanges.

- **Stablecoins:** Cryptocurrencies like DAI and USDC are pegged to stable assets, such as fiat currencies, providing a reliable medium for transactions.

- **Yield Farming:** Users can earn rewards by providing liquidity to DeFi protocols or participating in staking.

- **Insurance:** Decentralized insurance platforms, like Nexus Mutual, provide coverage against risks such as smart contract failures.

The DeFi ecosystem has grown rapidly since its inception, attracting billions of dollars in total value locked (TVL), a metric that represents the total assets committed to DeFi protocols. This growth underscores the increasing interest in decentralized financial services.

9.2. Popular DeFi Platforms and Applications

The rise of DeFi has given birth to a wide array of platforms and applications, each addressing specific financial needs. Below are some of the most popular and impactful ones:

1. Aave

Aave is a decentralized lending and borrowing platform that allows users to earn interest on deposits or borrow assets against collateral. It introduced innovative features like flash loans, which are uncollateralized loans that must be repaid within the same transaction.

2. Compound

Similar to Aave, Compound enables users to lend or borrow cryptocurrencies. Interest rates are dynamically adjusted based on supply and demand, and users earn COMP tokens for participating in the platform.

3. Uniswap

Uniswap is a decentralized exchange (DEX) that enables users to trade cryptocurrencies directly from their wallets. It uses an automated market maker (AMM) model, where liquidity pools replace traditional order books.

4. MakerDAO and DAI

MakerDAO is the protocol behind DAI, a decentralized stablecoin pegged to the US dollar. Users can lock Ethereum (ETH) or other assets as collateral in Maker Vaults to generate DAI.

5. Curve Finance

Curve is a DEX optimized for stablecoin trading. Its focus on minimizing slippage and fees makes it a popular choice for users looking to swap stablecoins efficiently.

6. Yearn.Finance

Yearn.Finance automates yield farming by optimizing user investments across various DeFi protocols. It simplifies complex strategies, making them accessible to everyday users.

7. Balancer

Balancer is a portfolio manager and liquidity provider that allows users to create customized token pools. These pools automatically rebalance based on predefined weightings.

8. SushiSwap

Initially a fork of Uniswap, SushiSwap has expanded its services to include yield farming, staking, and lending. It also offers community governance, allowing users to vote on protocol updates.

9. Nexus Mutual

Nexus Mutual provides decentralized insurance for smart contract failures and other risks. It operates as a mutual insurance company, where members share risks and benefits.

10. PancakeSwap

Built on the Binance Smart Chain, PancakeSwap offers lower transaction fees than Ethereum-based platforms. It supports trading, yield farming, and staking with a user-friendly interface.

These platforms represent just a fraction of the DeFi ecosystem, which continues to expand with innovative solutions. The diversity of applications ensures that users can find tailored services to meet their financial goals.

9.3. Risks and Rewards in DeFi

DeFi offers significant opportunities for financial inclusion and innovation, but it also comes with a unique set of risks. Understanding both the rewards and the challenges is crucial for anyone looking to participate in the DeFi space.

Rewards of DeFi:

1. Financial Inclusion: DeFi breaks down barriers to entry, allowing people worldwide to access financial services without traditional requirements.

2. High Yield Opportunities: Yield farming and liquidity provision can offer significantly higher returns than traditional savings accounts or investments.

3. Control Over Assets: Users retain full control of their funds, eliminating reliance on centralized institutions.

4. Transparency and Security: Blockchain technology ensures that transactions are traceable and secure.

5. Innovation and Flexibility: DeFi protocols are constantly evolving, offering diverse and innovative financial products.

Risks in DeFi

1. Smart Contract Vulnerabilities: Bugs or exploits in smart contracts can lead to significant losses. Auditing helps but doesn't guarantee complete safety.

2. Market Volatility: Cryptocurrencies are known for their price volatility, which can impact the value of assets locked in DeFi platforms.

3. Regulatory Uncertainty: DeFi operates in a legal gray area in many jurisdictions, posing potential compliance challenges.

4. Liquidity Risks: Low liquidity in certain pools can lead to slippage or difficulties in executing trades.

5. Impermanent Loss: Liquidity providers may face losses if the price of assets in a pool changes significantly.

6. Scams and Fraud: The lack of regulation has allowed fraudulent projects to proliferate, making due diligence essential.

Mitigating Risks:

- **Research:** Thoroughly research protocols before participating.

- **Diversification:** Spread investments across multiple platforms to reduce risk exposure.

- **Audits:** Choose platforms that have undergone rigorous security audits.

- **Small Allocations:** Start with small amounts to minimize potential losses.

The rise of Decentralized Finance (DeFi) marks a significant milestone in the evolution of financial systems. By leveraging blockchain technology and smart contracts, DeFi offers unparalleled opportunities for financial inclusion, transparency, and innovation. However, it also introduces risks that require careful consideration.

As DeFi continues to mature, its potential to reshape the global financial landscape becomes increasingly apparent. Whether you're a casual participant or an investor seeking new opportunities, understanding the foundations, platforms, and risks of DeFi is essential for navigating this transformative space.

PART 4: Technical and Practical Insights

10. Blockchain Technology in Depth

Blockchain technology has transformed the way we think about trust, transparency, and decentralized systems. At its core, blockchain is a distributed ledger system that records transactions across a network of computers in a way that is secure, transparent, and immutable. This chapter dives deeper into the mechanics of blockchain technology, focusing on two critical areas: consensus mechanisms and scaling challenges and solutions.

10.1. Understanding Consensus Mechanisms

A blockchain's success relies heavily on its ability to achieve consensus among its participants. Consensus mechanisms ensure that all nodes in the network agree on the state of the blockchain, even in the presence of malicious actors. This section explores the most widely used consensus mechanisms, including Proof of Work (PoW), Proof of Stake (PoS), and their variations.

Proof of Work (PoW)

Proof of Work is the original consensus mechanism introduced by Bitcoin. It requires network participants, called miners, to solve complex mathematical puzzles to validate transactions and add them to the blockchain.

How It Works:
Miners compete to solve a cryptographic puzzle. The first to solve it earns the right to add a new block to the chain and is rewarded with cryptocurrency. The puzzle's difficulty adjusts dynamically to maintain a consistent block production time.

Advantages:
- High security due to the computational power required to alter the blockchain.
- Decentralization: No single entity controls the network.

Disadvantages:
- High energy consumption.
- Limited transaction throughput.

Proof of Stake (PoS)

Proof of Stake is an energy-efficient alternative to PoW. Instead of solving puzzles, validators are chosen to create new blocks based on the number of coins they hold and are willing to "stake."

How It Works:

Validators lock up a certain amount of cryptocurrency as collateral. A randomized selection process determines who gets to validate transactions. Validators are rewarded with transaction fees or new coins.

Advantages:
- Low energy usage.
- Faster transaction processing.

Disadvantages:
- Potential centralization, as wealthier participants have more influence.
- Vulnerability to "nothing at stake" attacks, though mitigated by slashing mechanisms.

Delegated Proof of Stake (DPoS)

An evolution of PoS, DPoS uses a voting system where stakeholders elect a small group of validators to manage the blockchain.

Advantages:
- Higher scalability and efficiency.

- Democratic governance model.

Disadvantages:
- Risk of validator collusion.
- Reduced decentralization compared to PoW and PoS.

Other Consensus Mechanisms

1. Proof of Authority (PoA): Relies on trusted validators approved by the network. It's often used in private or consortium blockchains.

2. Practical Byzantine Fault Tolerance (PBFT): Designed for permissioned blockchains, ensuring consensus even when some nodes are malicious.

3. Hybrid Mechanisms: Many blockchains combine PoW and PoS for enhanced security and efficiency, such as Ethereum's transition to Ethereum 2.0.

Mechanism	Energy Efficiency	Scalability	Security	Use Cases
Proof of Work	Low	Low	High	Bitcoin, Litecoin
Proof of Stake	High	Medium	Medium to High	Ethereum 2.0, Cardano
Delegated PoS	High	High	Medium	EOS, TRON

Table 10.1. Comparing Consensus Mechanisms

10.2. Scaling Challenges and Solutions

As blockchain technology gains mainstream adoption, its scalability has become a critical challenge. Scalability refers to a blockchain's ability to handle a growing number of transactions without compromising performance. This section explores the key scalability issues and potential solutions.

Challenges in Blockchain Scalability

1. Low Transaction Throughput:

- **Bitcoin:** Processes around 7 transactions per second (TPS).
- **Ethereum (pre-2.0):** Handles roughly 15-30 TPS.

These figures pale in comparison to traditional systems like Visa, which processes over 24,000 TPS.

2. Latency:

- Block confirmation times can take several minutes (Bitcoin) or seconds (Ethereum), causing delays in transaction finality.

3. Resource Requirements:

- Blockchain nodes must store and validate all transactions, leading to significant computational and storage demands as the network grows.

4. Decentralization vs. Scalability:

- Solutions that improve scalability often require trade-offs with decentralization, as seen in some permissioned or delegated networks.

Solutions to Blockchain Scalability

On-Chain Solutions (Layer 1):

On-chain solutions involve improving the base layer of the blockchain to handle more transactions.

1. Sharding:
- The blockchain is divided into smaller, manageable parts called shards.
- Each shard processes transactions independently, increasing overall throughput.
- **Example:** Ethereum 2.0 plans to implement sharding.

2. Improved Consensus Mechanisms:
- Switching to faster and more efficient mechanisms like PoS or DPoS.
- **Example:** Ethereum's shift from PoW to PoS.

3. Block Size Increase:
- Larger blocks can store more transactions.
- **Example:** Bitcoin Cash increased its block size to 8 MB, compared to Bitcoin's 1 MB.

- **Drawbacks:** Larger blocks require more storage and bandwidth, raising centralization concerns.

Off-Chain Solutions (Layer 2):

Off-chain solutions process transactions outside the main blockchain, reducing the load on the base layer.

1. State Channels:
- Transactions occur off-chain between parties and are settled on-chain only when necessary.
- **Examples:** Bitcoin's Lightning Network, Ethereum's Raiden Network.

2. Sidechains:
- Independent blockchains connected to the main chain. Transactions are processed on sidechains and periodically synchronized with the main chain.
- **Examples:** Polygon (formerly Matic) for Ethereum.

3. Rollups:
- Bundle multiple transactions into a single batch and submit them to the main chain.

Types:
- Optimistic Rollups: Assume transactions are valid by default and only verify if challenged.

- Zero-Knowledge Rollups (ZK-Rollups): Use cryptographic proofs to validate transactions efficiently.

Hybrid Approaches:

Many projects combine Layer 1 and Layer 2 solutions for optimal scalability. For instance, Ethereum's roadmap includes both sharding (Layer 1) and rollups (Layer 2).

Real-World Applications and Examples

1. Bitcoin Lightning Network:
- Enables fast, low-cost microtransactions by settling most payments off-chain.
- **Benefits:** Near-instant payments, reduced fees.

2. Ethereum's Rollup Ecosystem:
- Rollup solutions like Optimism and Arbitrum handle smart contract transactions efficiently, allowing Ethereum to scale without sacrificing security.

3. Polkadot and Cosmos:
- Interoperable blockchain ecosystems that use parachains (sharded chains) to enhance scalability and connectivity.

Future of Blockchain Scalability

As blockchain technology evolves, scalability will remain a primary focus. Emerging technologies such as Layer 3 protocols, quantum-resistant algorithms, and AI-driven optimization promise to push the boundaries of what blockchains can achieve. Achieving the ideal balance between decentralization, security, and scalability—known as the blockchain trilemma—will be crucial in shaping the future of this technology.

This in-depth understanding of consensus mechanisms and scaling challenges and solutions highlights how blockchain technology continues to innovate and adapt to meet the demands of a growing user base. Whether through more efficient consensus models or cutting-edge scalability solutions, blockchains are paving the way for a decentralized and interconnected world.

11. The Role of Cryptography in Blockchain

Blockchain technology owes its security, reliability, and efficiency to cryptography. Cryptography is the backbone that ensures transactions on the blockchain are secure, data integrity is maintained, and trust is established in a trustless environment. Cryptographic methods enable blockchain to function as a decentralized and tamper-resistant ledger, making it a critical component of cryptocurrencies and other blockchain applications.

This chapter will explore the key aspects of cryptography in blockchain by focusing on two major concepts: Public and Private Keys and Hashing and Digital Signatures.

11.1. Public and Private Keys Explained

Public and private keys are foundational to blockchain technology, enabling secure transactions and identity verification. These keys are a part of asymmetric cryptography, a cryptographic system that uses a pair of keys for encryption and decryption. Understanding how they work is crucial to grasping the mechanics of blockchain.

11.1.1. Asymmetric Cryptography

In asymmetric cryptography, every participant in a blockchain network possesses two keys:

1. Public Key: This key is shared openly and can be distributed to others. It functions like an address where information can be sent.

2. Private Key: This key is kept secret and is used to decrypt data or sign transactions. It functions like a password that ensures the owner's control over their data or assets.

The public and private keys are mathematically linked. Data encrypted with the public key can only be decrypted using the corresponding private key, and vice versa. This relationship underpins the security of blockchain networks.

11.1.2. Key Generation

Keys are generated using algorithms such as RSA (Rivest-Shamir-Adleman) or Elliptic Curve Cryptography (ECC). These algorithms ensure the keys are computationally secure, meaning it's practically impossible to derive the private key from the public key.

For example, Bitcoin uses ECC with a specific algorithm called Secp256k1. This algorithm allows the generation of compact keys, enhancing efficiency without compromising security.

11.1.3. Role in Blockchain Transactions

Public and private keys play a crucial role in ensuring secure transactions:

Creating a Wallet: A blockchain wallet is essentially a pair of public and private keys. The public key serves as the wallet address, while the private key grants access to the funds.

Transaction Signing: When initiating a transaction, the sender uses their private key to sign it digitally. This signature serves as proof of ownership and authorization.

Verification: Nodes in the blockchain network verify the transaction by using the sender's public key to validate the signature. This process ensures the transaction's authenticity and integrity.

11.1.4. Importance of Private Key Security

The private key is the ultimate proof of ownership in a blockchain system. If it is lost or compromised, the associated funds or data cannot be recovered. This highlights the importance of secure key management, such as using hardware wallets, encrypted backups, or multi-signature wallets.

Example in Practice

When Alice sends Bitcoin to Bob, the process involves the following:

- 1. Alice uses her private key to sign the transaction.
- 2. The network validates the signature using Alice's public key.
- 3. Once validated, the transaction is added to the blockchain.

This system ensures that only Alice, the rightful owner of the private key, can authorize the transaction, and anyone can verify its authenticity using her public key.

11.2. Hashing and Digital Signatures

Hashing and digital signatures are cryptographic techniques that ensure data integrity, authenticity, and non-repudiation on the blockchain. These methods work together to secure transactions and maintain the blockchain's immutability.

11.2.1. What is Hashing?

Hashing is the process of converting input data of any size into a fixed-length string of characters, known as a hash. This process is performed using hash functions like SHA-256 (Secure Hash Algorithm 256-bit), which is commonly used in Bitcoin.

Properties of a Hash Function

1. Deterministic: The same input always produces the same output.

2. Fast Computation: Hashing an input is computationally efficient.

3. Pre-image Resistance: It is infeasible to derive the original input from its hash.

4. Small Changes in Input Produce Large Changes in Output: A slight alteration in input results in a completely different hash, ensuring data integrity.

5. Collision Resistance: It is extremely unlikely for two different inputs to produce the same hash.

Role of Hashing in Blockchain

1. Data Integrity: Each block in a blockchain contains a hash of the previous block. This chaining ensures that any change in a block alters its hash, invalidating the chain.

2. Proof of Work: In cryptocurrencies like Bitcoin, miners solve complex puzzles by finding a hash that meets specific criteria. This process secures the network.

3. Transaction Verification: Hashing ensures that transactions remain tamper-proof, as any modification will produce a different hash.

11.2.2. Digital Signatures

Digital signatures combine hashing and asymmetric cryptography to verify the authenticity of a transaction or message. They serve as proof that a specific individual signed a piece of data and that it hasn't been altered.

How Digital Signatures Work

1. Creating a Signature:

- The sender hashes the transaction data using a hash function.
- The hash is then encrypted with the sender's private key, creating the digital signature.

2. Verification:

- The recipient decrypts the signature using the sender's public key to retrieve the hash.
- The recipient independently hashes the transaction data and compares it with the decrypted hash. If they match, the signature is valid.

Benefits of Digital Signatures

- **Authentication:** Ensures that the sender is the true owner of the private key.
- **Integrity:** Confirms that the data hasn't been tampered with.
- **Non-repudiation:** Prevents the sender from denying their involvement in the transaction.

11.2.3. Application in Blockchain

1. Transaction Security: Every blockchain transaction is signed digitally, ensuring it originates from the rightful owner.

2. Smart Contracts: Digital signatures validate conditions and parties in smart contracts.

3. Consensus Mechanisms: Some blockchain protocols, like Proof of Stake (PoS), use digital signatures for verifying validators.

Example in Practice

Consider a blockchain-based document-sharing platform:

- When Alice shares a document with Bob, she signs it digitally using her private key.
- Bob verifies the signature using Alice's public key, ensuring that the document is authentic and untampered.

Combining Hashing and Digital Signatures

Hashing and digital signatures often work in tandem to secure blockchain systems. For instance:

- When a transaction is broadcast to the network, it is hashed.
- The hash is signed digitally by the sender.
- Validators use the sender's public key to verify the signature and the hash to check data integrity.

Cryptography is at the core of blockchain technology, enabling secure, transparent, and decentralized operations. Public and private keys ensure identity verification and transaction security, while hashing and digital signatures guarantee data integrity and authenticity. Together, these cryptographic techniques create a robust system that underpins the success of cryptocurrencies and other blockchain applications.

By mastering the principles of cryptography, one can better understand the inner workings of blockchain and appreciate its potential to revolutionize industries.

12. The Future of Blockchain Technology

The blockchain revolution is still in its infancy, and its potential to reshape industries, economies, and societies is immense. While it began as the underlying technology for Bitcoin, blockchain has grown into a powerful tool for decentralization, security, and transparency across various sectors. In this chapter, we explore how blockchain is revolutionizing key industries like healthcare and supply chain, and delve into the emerging trends that promise to redefine the digital landscape, such as Non-Fungible Tokens (NFTs), Web3, and the Metaverse.

12.1. Blockchain in Industries: Healthcare, Supply Chain, and More

Healthcare

Blockchain is poised to revolutionize healthcare by addressing critical challenges such as data security, interoperability, and patient privacy. Traditional healthcare systems struggle with fragmented data silos and vulnerabilities to cyberattacks. Blockchain offers a secure, transparent, and decentralized way to store and share medical records.

1. Secure Patient Data

Blockchain ensures patient data remains tamper-proof by using cryptographic hashing. Each record is stored as a block in the chain, making it immutable. Patients have control over their records, granting access only to authorized entities, which strengthens privacy while adhering to regulations like HIPAA.

2. Improved Interoperability

Interoperability is a significant issue in healthcare. Blockchain creates a unified system where multiple healthcare providers can access a patient's medical history securely and seamlessly. This can lead to more accurate diagnoses, fewer redundancies, and better-coordinated care.

3. Combatting Counterfeit Drugs

The pharmaceutical industry loses billions annually to counterfeit drugs. Blockchain provides end-to-end traceability of drugs, from manufacturers to consumers, ensuring authenticity and reducing risks to public health.

Supply Chain

The supply chain is another sector experiencing a blockchain revolution. Traditional supply chain management is fraught with inefficiencies, fraud, and lack of transparency. Blockchain enhances trust and accountability by creating a transparent and immutable ledger of transactions.

1. Enhanced Transparency

Blockchain records every transaction in the supply chain, from raw material sourcing to final delivery. Stakeholders can trace a product's journey, ensuring compliance with ethical and sustainability standards. For example, consumers can verify if their coffee beans are sourced from fair trade farms.

2. Fraud Prevention

Counterfeit goods are a pervasive problem in industries like luxury goods, electronics, and food. Blockchain's tamper-proof records ensure the authenticity of products, protecting brands and consumers alike.

3. Efficiency Gains

By automating processes through smart contracts, blockchain reduces paperwork, manual errors, and transaction times. For instance, customs clearance can be expedited using blockchain-enabled systems.

Other Key Industries

1. Finance

Beyond cryptocurrencies, blockchain is transforming traditional finance by enabling faster cross-border payments, reducing transaction fees, and enhancing security. Decentralized finance (DeFi) platforms allow users to borrow, lend, and trade without intermediaries, democratizing access to financial services.

2. Real Estate

Blockchain simplifies property transactions by digitizing titles and automating processes through smart contracts. This reduces fraud and accelerates transactions, making real estate more accessible.

3. Energy

Blockchain supports decentralized energy grids, enabling peer-to-peer energy trading. Homeowners with solar panels can sell excess power directly to their neighbors using blockchain-based platforms.

12.2. Emerging Trends: NFTs, Web3, and the Metaverse

The blockchain landscape is rapidly evolving, giving rise to groundbreaking trends that are reshaping digital experiences and economies.

NFTs (Non-Fungible Tokens)

NFTs are unique digital assets stored on a blockchain, representing ownership of art, music, videos, and even virtual real estate. Unlike cryptocurrencies, which are fungible (interchangeable), NFTs are one-of-a-kind.

1. Revolutionizing Art and Entertainment

NFTs have disrupted traditional art markets by enabling artists to sell directly to buyers without intermediaries. Digital artists can embed royalties in their NFTs, earning a percentage of sales each time their work is resold.

2. Gaming and Virtual Goods

NFTs are transforming gaming by allowing players to own and trade in-game assets like skins, weapons, and characters. Games like Axie Infinity have pioneered play-to-earn models, where players earn cryptocurrency rewards.

3. Tokenizing Real-World Assets

NFTs extend beyond digital art. Real-world assets, such as real estate, luxury items, and collectibles, can be tokenized as NFTs, allowing fractional ownership and increased liquidity.

Web3

Web3 represents the next generation of the internet, built on blockchain technology to create a decentralized, user-centric ecosystem. It seeks to address the flaws of Web2, such as data monopolization and lack of user privacy.

1. Decentralized Applications (DApps)

Web3 enables the creation of DApps, which run on decentralized networks rather than centralized servers. These applications, ranging from social media to finance, prioritize user control and data privacy.

2. Self-Sovereign Identity

Web3 gives users ownership of their digital identities. Instead of relying on centralized entities like Facebook or Google for authentication, users can control their data through blockchain-based solutions.

3. Decentralized Autonomous Organizations (DAOs)

DAOs are blockchain-based organizations governed by smart contracts and community voting. They eliminate the need for traditional hierarchical management structures, empowering members to make collective decisions.

The Metaverse

The metaverse is an immersive virtual world where users can interact, socialize, and transact using digital avatars. Blockchain plays a crucial role in enabling a decentralized and interoperable metaverse.

1. Digital Ownership and Economy

Blockchain allows users to own virtual assets, such as land, clothing, and experiences, as NFTs. This creates a thriving economy where users can buy, sell, and trade assets across different platforms.

2. Interoperability

Blockchain ensures that digital assets can move seamlessly across different metaverse platforms. For example, an avatar's outfit purchased in one virtual world can be used in another.

3. Decentralized Governance

Just as DAOs democratize decision-making, blockchain enables users to participate in governing the metaverse, ensuring it remains community-driven and equitable.

Challenges and Opportunities

While these trends are exciting, they also come with challenges. Scalability, energy consumption, and regulatory uncertainty remain significant hurdles. However, ongoing advancements in blockchain technology, such as Layer 2 solutions and green blockchain initiatives, are addressing these issues.

The future of blockchain technology is brimming with potential. From transforming industries like healthcare and supply chain to pioneering trends like NFTs, Web3, and the metaverse, blockchain is reshaping the world as we know it. While challenges exist, the relentless pace of innovation ensures that blockchain will continue to drive progress in the digital age, empowering individuals and industries alike.

PART 5: Challenges and Opportunities

13. Regulations and Legal Implications

The rapid rise of cryptocurrencies and blockchain technology has not only disrupted traditional financial systems but also challenged existing regulatory frameworks worldwide. This chapter explores global regulatory perspectives and the legal challenges faced in blockchain adoption. Understanding these implications is crucial for businesses, developers, and users aiming to navigate the complexities of this transformative technology.

13.1. Global Perspectives on Cryptocurrency Regulation

Cryptocurrencies emerged in a largely unregulated space, leading to a wide range of approaches by governments and regulatory bodies. Some nations have embraced digital assets, recognizing their potential for innovation and economic growth, while others have imposed strict restrictions, citing concerns over financial stability, security, and illicit activities.

The United States

The U.S. approach to cryptocurrency regulation is fragmented, with different agencies overseeing various aspects.

The SEC (Securities and Exchange Commission):

Focuses on whether cryptocurrencies qualify as securities. The SEC has taken action against Initial Coin Offerings (ICOs) that fail to comply with securities laws.

The CFTC (Commodity Futures Trading Commission): Treats cryptocurrencies like Bitcoin as commodities, regulating derivatives markets.

The IRS (Internal Revenue Service): Classifies cryptocurrencies as property for tax purposes, requiring reporting of gains and losses.

The U.S. regulatory environment remains ambiguous, creating challenges for businesses seeking clarity.

The European Union

The EU has taken a more unified approach through its Markets in Crypto-Assets Regulation (MiCA) framework, set to come into effect in 2025.

Key Features of MiCA:

- Licensing requirements for crypto-asset service providers.
- Consumer protection measures.
- Clear rules for stablecoins.

Individual member states, such as Germany and France, have also implemented their own regulations, but MiCA aims to harmonize these efforts across the region.

Asia

China: Adopted a hardline stance by banning cryptocurrency trading and mining in 2021. However, the country is actively developing its own Digital Yuan, showcasing its interest in blockchain's potential for centralized digital currencies.

Japan: One of the first countries to regulate cryptocurrencies, recognizing Bitcoin as legal tender and requiring exchanges to register with the Financial Services Agency (FSA).

India: The government has oscillated between imposing strict regulations and embracing the technology. A proposed digital rupee indicates a growing interest in blockchain-backed solutions.

Other Regions

- **Africa:** Countries like Nigeria and Kenya have high cryptocurrency adoption rates but face regulatory uncertainty. Some governments are exploring blockchain for digital identity and financial inclusion.
- **South America:** Nations like El Salvador have fully embraced cryptocurrencies, with Bitcoin being adopted as legal tender, while others remain cautious.

Common Challenges in Global Regulation

- **Lack of Consistency:** Differing regulatory approaches create uncertainty for businesses operating across borders.

- **AML (Anti-Money Laundering) and KYC (Know Your Customer):** Ensuring compliance without compromising user privacy.

- **Decentralization:** The anonymous and borderless nature of blockchain makes enforcement difficult.

Future Trends in Cryptocurrency Regulation

As the market matures, we can expect more comprehensive and harmonized regulations. Regulatory sandboxes, international cooperation, and technological advancements may address existing gaps and pave the way for a more stable regulatory environment.

13.2. Legal Challenges in Blockchain Adoption

While blockchain technology offers significant advantages in transparency, security, and efficiency, its adoption is fraught with legal hurdles. These challenges span various sectors, including finance, healthcare, and supply chain management.

1. Jurisdictional Issues

Blockchain's decentralized nature makes it difficult to determine which legal jurisdiction applies in disputes.

For example:

- If a smart contract is executed between parties in different countries, whose laws govern the transaction?

- How can cross-border enforcement be managed when blockchain nodes operate globally?

Solutions like international treaties or blockchain-specific arbitration frameworks may help address these issues.

2. Data Privacy and Protection

The immutability of blockchain records poses challenges under data protection laws like the General Data Protection Regulation (GDPR) in the EU. Key conflicts include:

- **Right to Be Forgotten:** Blockchain's design prevents data deletion, conflicting with GDPR's requirement to allow individuals to erase their personal data.

- **Data Ownership:** Determining who owns and controls data on public blockchains is complex.

Innovations like zero-knowledge proofs and private blockchains may offer solutions by enabling compliance without compromising blockchain's integrity.

3. Intellectual Property Rights

Blockchain-based innovations often involve intellectual property (IP) disputes:

- Who owns the rights to smart contracts or decentralized applications (DApps)?
- How can copyright and patents be enforced in open-source blockchain ecosystems?

Collaboration between developers and legal experts is essential to address these challenges.

4. Smart Contracts and Legal Recognition

Smart contracts, self-executing agreements coded on blockchain, are not universally recognized as legally binding. Key issues include:

- **Ambiguity:** Code is open to interpretation, and errors can lead to disputes.

- **Enforceability:** Courts may lack the technical expertise to interpret or enforce smart contracts.

Efforts are underway to integrate smart contracts into traditional legal frameworks, ensuring they align with existing contract laws.

5. Liability and Accountability

In a decentralized network, determining liability is challenging:

- Who is responsible for errors in a smart contract?
- If a decentralized autonomous organization (DAO) causes harm, how is accountability assigned?

Clear guidelines and frameworks are needed to address these issues, particularly as DAOs become more prominent.

6. Financial Crimes and Security Risks

Blockchain's anonymity is a double-edged sword, enabling both privacy and potential misuse:

- Cryptocurrencies have been linked to money laundering, ransomware, and other illicit activities.
- Regulatory bodies are working to integrate blockchain into AML and KYC processes.

Blockchain analytics firms are also developing tools to trace and identify suspicious activities while preserving user privacy.

7. Token Classification and Regulation

The rise of ICOs and tokenized assets has raised questions about classification:

- Are tokens securities, commodities, or something else entirely?
- Misclassification can lead to regulatory penalties and investor losses.

Standardized definitions and regulatory clarity are essential to encourage innovation while protecting stakeholders.

8. Ethical and Environmental Concerns

Blockchain adoption raises ethical and environmental issues:

- **Energy Consumption:** Proof-of-Work (PoW) blockchains like Bitcoin are energy-intensive, leading to environmental concerns.
- **Inequality:** Blockchain's accessibility issues could widen the digital divide.

Regulators and businesses must address these concerns to ensure sustainable adoption.

Emerging Solutions and Legal Trends

- **RegTech (Regulatory Technology):** Automating compliance processes using blockchain itself.
- **Self-Regulation:** Industry-led initiatives to establish ethical and operational standards.
- **Public-Private Partnerships:** Governments and blockchain developers collaborating to address legal and regulatory challenges.

The intersection of blockchain technology and legal systems is both challenging and promising. While regulatory clarity and legal frameworks are still evolving, addressing these challenges is critical for unlocking blockchain's full potential. By fostering collaboration between technologists, regulators, and legal experts, we can ensure blockchain adoption in a way that is innovative, ethical, and secure.

14. Environmental Impact of Cryptocurrencies

The environmental impact of cryptocurrencies, particularly Bitcoin and blockchain technologies, has become a highly debated topic. While the transformative potential of blockchain is undeniable, its energy-intensive processes, such as mining, raise questions about sustainability. This chapter delves into the environmental concerns associated with cryptocurrencies, with a particular focus on energy consumption in Bitcoin mining and emerging sustainable blockchain solutions.

14.1. Energy Consumption and Bitcoin Mining

Bitcoin mining is the process by which transactions are validated and added to the blockchain. It relies on a consensus mechanism called Proof of Work (PoW), which requires miners to solve complex mathematical problems. This process ensures the security and decentralization of the network but comes at a significant energy cost.

The Mechanics of Bitcoin Mining

Bitcoin mining involves specialized hardware known as **Application-Specific Integrated Circuits (ASICs)**, which are designed to perform the hashing algorithms necessary for mining. These machines run continuously, consuming vast amounts of electricity. As the Bitcoin network grows, the difficulty of mining increases, requiring even more computational power and energy.

The Energy Debate

A key criticism of Bitcoin is its energy consumption. The Bitcoin network reportedly uses more electricity annually than some small countries, such as Argentina or the Netherlands. The Cambridge Bitcoin Electricity Consumption Index (CBECI) estimates Bitcoin's energy usage to be around 120 terawatt-hours (TWh) per year, which has raised alarm among environmental advocates.

Fossil Fuels and Mining

A large portion of Bitcoin mining is powered by non-renewable energy sources, such as coal and natural gas, particularly in regions like China (until its mining ban in 2021), Kazakhstan, and Russia. This reliance on fossil fuels contributes to greenhouse gas emissions, making Bitcoin mining a contributor to climate change.

Geographical Concentration of Miners

The environmental impact of Bitcoin mining is influenced by the geographical location of mining operations. For instance:

- **China (pre-ban)**: Coal-powered mining operations in China accounted for a significant portion of the network's energy consumption.
- **Kazakhstan**: After China's mining ban, many miners relocated to Kazakhstan, where coal remains a primary energy source.
- **United States**: The U.S. has seen a surge in mining operations, with some leveraging renewable energy, but others relying on fossil fuels.

Economic vs. Environmental Costs

While Bitcoin mining has economic benefits, such as job creation and financial inclusion, the environmental costs are considerable. The balance between these factors is a critical challenge for the cryptocurrency industry.

14.2. Sustainable Blockchain Solutions

The environmental challenges of cryptocurrencies have sparked innovation, with many stakeholders exploring sustainable alternatives to energy-intensive blockchain technologies. Below, we explore some of the most promising solutions.

Transitioning from Proof of Work (PoW) to Proof of Stake (PoS)

One of the most significant shifts in blockchain technology is the move from PoW to Proof of Stake (PoS). Unlike PoW, which requires miners to solve computational puzzles, PoS selects validators based on the number of coins they hold and are willing to "stake" as collateral. This dramatically reduces energy consumption.

- **Ethereum's Transition**: In 2022, Ethereum transitioned from PoW to PoS through an upgrade known as "The Merge." This change reduced Ethereum's energy consumption by approximately 99.95%, setting a precedent for other blockchains.
- **Advantages of PoS**:
    - Energy efficiency: No need for extensive hardware or continuous electricity.
    - Accessibility: Lower barrier to entry for participation in the network.
    - Scalability: PoS systems can process transactions faster.

Renewable Energy and Green Mining

Some mining operations are pivoting toward renewable energy sources, such as solar, wind, and hydroelectric power. For example:

- **Iceland**: Many Bitcoin miners in Iceland use geothermal and hydroelectric power, which are abundant and renewable.
- **Texas, USA**: With its vast wind farms, Texas has become a hub for eco-friendly Bitcoin mining.

Carbon Offset Initiatives

To mitigate environmental damage, some cryptocurrency projects are investing in carbon offset programs. These initiatives aim to counterbalance emissions by funding projects such as reforestation and renewable energy development.

- **Companies Leading the Charge**: Several mining firms, including Argo Blockchain and Marathon Digital Holdings, have pledged to become carbon-neutral by investing in offsets.

Layer 2 Scaling Solutions

Layer 2 solutions aim to reduce the energy and computational load on blockchain networks. These solutions process transactions off-chain and later record them on the main blockchain, improving efficiency.

- **Lightning Network**: For Bitcoin, the Lightning Network enables faster and cheaper transactions by processing them off-chain, reducing the energy demands of the main network.

Hybrid and Alternative Consensus Mechanisms

Innovative consensus mechanisms are being developed to balance security, decentralization, and sustainability. Examples include:

- **Proof of Authority (PoA)**: Relies on trusted validators, reducing computational requirements.
- **Delegated Proof of Stake (DPoS)**: Similar to PoS but with elected validators, making it more efficient.

Blockchain Projects Prioritizing Sustainability

Several blockchain projects are designed with sustainability in mind:

- **Algorand**: Marketed as a "carbon-negative" blockchain, Algorand uses a PoS mechanism and offsets its emissions.
- **Cardano**: Operates on a PoS system and emphasizes energy efficiency.

- **Chia Network**: Introduced a "Proof of Space and Time" mechanism, which uses storage capacity rather than computational power, significantly reducing energy consumption.

Regulatory and Community Initiatives

Governments and blockchain communities are also playing a role in fostering sustainable practices.

- **Energy Regulations**: Some governments are introducing policies to encourage green mining. For example, Sweden has proposed banning PoW mining in favor of more sustainable methods.
- **Community Awareness**: Advocacy groups within the crypto community, such as the Crypto Climate Accord, are pushing for the industry to achieve net-zero emissions by 2030.

The Path Forward

While cryptocurrencies and blockchains have undeniable potential to revolutionize industries, their environmental impact cannot be ignored. The shift towards sustainable practices, including PoS adoption, renewable energy usage, and innovative consensus mechanisms, offers a path to minimize their carbon footprint. However, achieving widespread adoption of these solutions will require collaboration among governments, blockchain developers, miners, and the broader community.

As the industry matures, balancing innovation with environmental stewardship will be critical to ensuring that cryptocurrencies and blockchain technologies contribute to a sustainable future. The journey toward eco-friendly blockchain solutions is not just an environmental imperative but also a necessity for the long-term viability and public acceptance of this transformative technology.

15. Investing in Cryptocurrencies

Cryptocurrencies have grown from a niche financial concept into a global investment phenomenon. While Bitcoin led the way, thousands of cryptocurrencies now offer a diverse range of applications and potential profits. However, the volatility and complexity of the market necessitate a solid understanding of its dynamics before diving in. This chapter explores how to invest wisely, balancing risks and rewards, diversifying your portfolio, and recognizing long-term trends that could shape the future of crypto investing.

15.1. Understanding Risks and Rewards

Investing in cryptocurrencies can be highly rewarding but equally risky. Unlike traditional investments, crypto markets operate 24/7 and are influenced by factors ranging from technological developments to regulatory news.

Risks of Investing in Cryptocurrencies

1. **Volatility:** Cryptocurrencies are infamous for their price swings. Bitcoin, for instance, has experienced price spikes of over 1,000% in a year and subsequent crashes. While this volatility creates opportunities for profit, it also exposes investors to significant losses.

2. **Regulatory Uncertainty:** Cryptocurrencies operate in a largely unregulated environment. Governments worldwide are still figuring out how to tax, regulate, or integrate these assets. Sudden regulatory changes, such as bans or tax hikes, can drastically impact the market.

3. **Security Concerns:** Hacking incidents, fraud, and theft are common in the crypto world. If not stored securely, your digital assets can be stolen, as seen in the infamous Mt. Gox hack in 2014.

4. **Market Manipulation:** Due to relatively low liquidity compared to traditional markets, cryptocurrency prices can be manipulated by whales (investors holding large amounts of a

cryptocurrency) or coordinated pump-and-dump schemes.

5. **Technological Risks:** Blockchain networks are robust, but they are not immune to technological failures, forks, or vulnerabilities in smart contracts, which could lead to loss of funds.

Rewards of Investing in Cryptocurrencies

1. **High Returns Potential:** Cryptocurrencies have generated unparalleled returns. Early Bitcoin investors saw their investments multiply thousands of times. Similarly, altcoins like Ethereum, Solana, and Binance Coin have delivered significant gains.

2. **Decentralized Opportunities:** Cryptocurrencies allow individuals to participate in financial systems without intermediaries like banks or governments. This decentralization opens up investment opportunities for anyone with an internet connection.

3. **Innovation and Growth:** Cryptocurrencies are at the forefront of technological innovation. By investing early in promising blockchain projects, investors can benefit from the growth of industries such as decentralized finance (DeFi)

and non-fungible tokens (NFTs).

4. **Hedge Against Inflation:** With limited supply and deflationary mechanisms, cryptocurrencies like Bitcoin are often viewed as digital gold, offering protection against inflation.

15.2. Diversifying Your Crypto Portfolio

Diversification is a fundamental principle in investment strategy. In the cryptocurrency market, diversification helps reduce risks associated with individual coins while increasing exposure to various growth opportunities.

Why Diversify?

1. **Mitigating Risk**: Different cryptocurrencies have varying use cases, market dynamics, and levels of risk. Diversification ensures that the failure of one coin doesn't significantly impact your overall portfolio.

2. **Maximizing Potential**: While Bitcoin and Ethereum dominate the market, smaller cryptocurrencies, often referred to as altcoins, may offer higher returns due to their growth potential.

3. **Exploring Use Cases**: By investing in a range of coins, you can participate in different sectors, such as DeFi, NFTs, gaming, and blockchain infrastructure.

How to Build a Diversified Portfolio

1. **Include Market Leaders**

    o Start with established cryptocurrencies like Bitcoin and Ethereum. These coins are less volatile compared to smaller altcoins and are considered safer investments.

2. **Explore Altcoins**

    o Look for promising altcoins with strong development teams, use cases, and market adoption. Examples include Solana (high-speed blockchain), Chainlink (oracle services), and Cardano (scalable smart contracts).

3. **Allocate to Stablecoins**

    o Stablecoins like USDT or USDC are pegged to fiat currencies and help provide stability to your portfolio, especially during market downturns.

4. **Participate in Emerging Trends**

    o Invest in newer sectors like metaverse tokens (e.g., Decentraland's MANA), decentralized finance projects (e.g., Aave), or layer-2 scaling solutions (e.g., Polygon).

5. **Limit Speculative Investments**

    o Allocate a small percentage of your portfolio to highly speculative coins with high-risk, high-reward potential. Conduct thorough research before investing.

Balancing Your Portfolio

- **Risk Tolerance**: Adjust your portfolio based on your risk appetite. Conservative investors may lean more towards Bitcoin and stablecoins, while aggressive investors may opt for a higher percentage of altcoins.
- **Rebalancing**: Regularly review and adjust your portfolio to maintain your desired asset allocation.
- **Geographic Diversification**: Consider projects from different regions to benefit from varying regulatory and technological environments.

Tools for Managing Your Portfolio

1. **Portfolio Trackers**: Use apps like CoinMarketCap, Delta, or Blockfolio to monitor your holdings and market trends.
2. **Hardware Wallets**: Secure your portfolio with hardware wallets like Ledger or Trezor to protect against theft.
3. **Research Platforms**: Websites like Messari, Glassnode, and CoinGecko provide data-driven insights to inform your investment decisions.

15.3. Long-Term Trends in Crypto Investing

Cryptocurrencies are still in their infancy, with immense potential for growth and transformation. Understanding long-term trends can help you position your investments to capitalize on future opportunities.

1. Institutional Adoption

Over the past few years, institutional interest in cryptocurrencies has skyrocketed. Major companies like Tesla and MicroStrategy have added Bitcoin to their balance sheets, while asset managers like BlackRock have launched crypto-related products. Institutional adoption provides legitimacy and increases liquidity, potentially stabilizing the market over time.

2. Expansion of Decentralized Finance (DeFi)

DeFi is revolutionizing traditional financial systems by offering services like lending, borrowing, and trading without intermediaries. Platforms like Uniswap, Aave, and Compound are leading this movement, which is expected to grow exponentially.

3. Growth of Layer-2 Solutions

Scalability remains a major challenge for blockchains like Ethereum. Layer-2 solutions such as Arbitrum, Optimism, and zkSync aim to reduce transaction costs and increase speeds, making blockchain technology more accessible.

4. Integration with Traditional Finance

As governments and financial institutions recognize the potential of blockchain, hybrid systems combining traditional and decentralized finance are emerging. Examples include central bank digital currencies (CBDCs) and blockchain-based settlement systems.

5. Increasing Regulation

While regulation can create uncertainty in the short term, it also provides clarity and protection for investors in the long term. Governments worldwide are working on frameworks to regulate cryptocurrencies, making the market more secure and attractive to mainstream investors.

6. Interoperability Between Blockchains

The future of blockchain lies in interoperability, enabling different blockchains to communicate and share data seamlessly. Projects like Polkadot and Cosmos are at the forefront of this trend.

7. Environmental Sustainability

Criticism over the environmental impact of cryptocurrencies like Bitcoin has led to the rise of eco-friendly alternatives. Ethereum's transition to proof-of-stake (PoS) is a major milestone in creating more energy-efficient blockchains.

8. Tokenization of Assets

Real-world assets, including real estate, stocks, and art, are being tokenized on the blockchain. This trend democratizes access to traditionally illiquid markets, opening up new investment opportunities.

9. Evolution of NFTs

Non-fungible tokens (NFTs) have moved beyond art and collectibles into areas like gaming, music, and virtual real estate. Their growth signifies the expanding scope of blockchain technology.

10. Global Economic Shifts

In regions with unstable economies, cryptocurrencies are increasingly seen as a hedge against inflation and currency devaluation. This trend will likely continue as more people turn to crypto for financial independence.

Investing in cryptocurrencies offers immense opportunities but requires a well-informed and disciplined approach. By understanding the risks and rewards, diversifying your portfolio, and staying attuned to long-term trends, you can navigate the volatile yet exciting world of crypto investing. Remember, thorough research, risk management, and patience are your best allies on this journey.

PART 6: Getting Started

16. Step-by-Step Guide to Your First Bitcoin

The world of Bitcoin can seem intimidating at first, but taking your first steps doesn't have to be complicated. This chapter walks you through acquiring and safely storing your first Bitcoin, ensuring a secure and seamless experience.

16.1. Choosing the Right Wallet

Your Bitcoin wallet is your gateway to interacting with the cryptocurrency world. It is crucial to choose the right wallet to ensure both security and ease of use.

What is a Bitcoin Wallet?

A Bitcoin wallet is a digital tool that allows you to send, receive, and store Bitcoin. It contains private keys that grant access to your funds and enables transactions on the blockchain. Wallets come in various forms, each with its own advantages and disadvantages.

Types of Bitcoin Wallets

1. Hardware Wallets

Hardware wallets are physical devices that store your private keys offline. They are among the most secure options available because they are immune to online threats like hacking. Popular hardware wallets include Ledger Nano X and Trezor.

2. Software Wallets

Software wallets are applications that you can download on your computer or smartphone. They are convenient but may be less secure than hardware wallets because they are connected to the internet. Examples include Electrum, Exodus, and Mycelium.

3. Web Wallets

Web wallets are hosted online and can be accessed through a browser. They are easy to use but are considered less secure since they rely on a third-party service provider. Examples include Blockchain.com and Coinbase.

4. Paper Wallets

Paper wallets involve printing your private and public keys on a piece of paper. While they are completely offline and secure from hacking, they are vulnerable to physical damage and loss.

5. Mobile Wallets

Mobile wallets are apps designed specifically for smartphones. They are great for on-the-go transactions but may not offer the same level of security as hardware wallets. Examples include Trust Wallet and BRD.

How to Choose the Right Wallet for You

Security Needs

If security is your top priority, opt for a hardware wallet. These wallets keep your private keys offline, reducing the risk of cyberattacks.

Frequency of Use

For frequent transactions, a mobile or software wallet might be more convenient.

Ease of Use

Beginners often find web wallets or user-friendly software wallets to be the easiest to navigate.

Cost

Hardware wallets typically cost between $50 and $200, while most software and web wallets are free to use.

Setting Up Your Wallet

1. Download and Install

Visit the official website of the wallet provider to download the software. For hardware wallets, follow the setup guide included in the package.

2. Create a New Wallet

Follow the on-screen instructions to create a new wallet.

3. Back Up Your Seed Phrase

Most wallets generate a recovery seed phrase during setup. Write it down and store it in a secure location. Never share this phrase with anyone.

4. Set Up Security Features

Enable additional security features like two-factor authentication (2FA) or a PIN code.

16.2 Safely Purchasing and Storing Bitcoin

After setting up your wallet, the next step is acquiring your first Bitcoin. This process involves choosing a reliable exchange and following best practices for secure storage.

Steps to Buy Bitcoin

1. Choose a Trusted Exchange

An exchange is a platform where you can buy and sell Bitcoin. Some of the most popular and reliable exchanges include:

- Coinbase
- Binance
- Kraken
- Bitstamp

When choosing an exchange, consider factors like security, fees, and user interface.

2. Create an Account

- Visit the exchange's website and click on "Sign Up."
- Provide your email address and create a strong password.

- Verify your email by clicking the link sent to your inbox.

3. Complete Identity Verification (KYC)

Most exchanges require you to complete a Know Your Customer (KYC) process. This typically involves submitting:

- A government-issued ID (e.g., passport or driver's license)
- Proof of address (e.g., utility bill or bank statement)

4. Deposit Funds

- Link your bank account or credit card to the exchange.
- Deposit your local currency to your exchange account.

5. Buy Bitcoin

- Navigate to the "Buy/Sell" section of the exchange.
- Enter the amount of Bitcoin you wish to purchase.
- Review the transaction details, including fees, and confirm your purchase.

Transferring Bitcoin to Your Wallet

Leaving your Bitcoin on an exchange can expose it to hacking risks. Transfer your Bitcoin to your wallet for safekeeping:

1. Copy Your Wallet Address

- Open your wallet app and locate your unique Bitcoin receiving address.

2. Initiate the Transfer

- In the exchange, go to the "Withdraw" section, paste your wallet address, and specify the amount to transfer.

3. Confirm the Transfer

- Review the transaction details and confirm. The Bitcoin should appear in your wallet shortly.

Best Practices for Storing Bitcoin

1. Use Cold Storage

Store your Bitcoin in a hardware or paper wallet to keep it offline and protected from hackers.

2. Enable Two-Factor Authentication

- Use 2FA to add an extra layer of security to your wallet and exchange accounts.

3. Regularly Back Up Your Wallet

Keep a secure backup of your wallet's seed phrase or private keys in multiple safe locations.

4. Avoid Public Wi-Fi

- When accessing your wallet or making transactions, avoid using public Wi-Fi networks to minimize the risk of interception.

5. Monitor Your Holdings

Regularly check your wallet balance and transaction history to spot any unauthorized activity.

Understanding Bitcoin Fees

When purchasing or transferring Bitcoin, you may encounter fees, such as:

Exchange Fees: Charged by the platform for buying and selling Bitcoin.

Network Fees: Paid to miners for processing Bitcoin transactions.

Being aware of these fees helps you plan and optimize your transactions.

Buying and storing Bitcoin is a straightforward process when broken down into manageable steps. By choosing the right wallet, selecting a trusted exchange, and following best practices, you can securely own and manage your first Bitcoin. As you become more familiar with Bitcoin, you'll gain confidence in navigating this exciting digital asset.

17. Building Your Knowledge and Skills

The cryptocurrency and blockchain world evolves at an astonishing pace. Staying informed and building your expertise in this field requires dedication and access to the right resources. This chapter focuses on helping you find reliable sources for deepening your understanding and strategies for staying updated in such a dynamic industry.

17.1. Reliable Resources for Learning More

When diving deeper into Bitcoin, blockchain, and cryptocurrencies, you need credible and up-to-date information. With the internet flooded with content, distinguishing reliable sources from questionable ones can be challenging. Below are key categories of trustworthy resources:

1. Books

Books are excellent for comprehensive understanding and foundational knowledge. Some widely respected titles include:

1. Mastering Bitcoin by Andreas M. Antonopoulos: A detailed technical guide to Bitcoin.

2. The Bitcoin Standard by Saifedean Ammous: A historical and economic perspective on Bitcoin.

3. Blockchain Basics by Daniel Drescher: A non-technical explanation of blockchain technology.

Books provide timeless insights, and many are written by industry pioneers. Look for updated editions or newly released titles to keep up with recent developments.

2. Online Courses and Tutorials

E-learning platforms offer structured courses tailored to different skill levels.

Coursera: Offers courses like Bitcoin and Cryptocurrency Technologies by Princeton University.

Udemy: Features numerous beginner-friendly courses such as Blockchain and Bitcoin Fundamentals.

LinkedIn Learning: Provides content on blockchain applications and cryptocurrency investments.

edX: Universities like MIT and Berkeley offer blockchain-focused modules here.

These platforms often combine video lessons with practical exercises, making it easier to grasp complex concepts.

3. Industry Websites and Blogs

Several trusted websites and blogs provide detailed articles, tutorials, and news:

- **CoinDesk:** A go-to source for blockchain news, insights, and analysis.
- **CryptoSlate:** Offers news and information on cryptocurrencies and blockchain.
- **Medium:** Look for posts from credible authors or organizations in the crypto space.
- **Bitcoin.org:** The official Bitcoin website contains guides and links to technical resources.

4. Research Papers and Whitepapers

For those interested in the technical and academic aspects, research papers and whitepapers are invaluable.

1. Bitcoin Whitepaper by Satoshi Nakamoto: A must-read for understanding Bitcoin's foundation.

2. Ethereum Whitepaper: Explains Ethereum's blockchain and smart contract concepts.

3. Websites like arXiv.org and SSRN.com host scholarly research on blockchain advancements.

5. Forums and Online Communities

Engaging with online communities allows you to learn from experienced users and discuss emerging trends.

- **BitcoinTalk:** The oldest and most popular Bitcoin forum.
- **Reddit:** Subreddits like r/Bitcoin, r/cryptocurrency, and r/ethdev are rich with discussions and resources.
- **Telegram and Discord Groups:** Many blockchain projects have active groups where members share updates and ideas.

However, always verify information from forums, as they can sometimes spread unverified claims.

6. Podcasts and YouTube Channels

Audio and visual content are great for on-the-go learning.

Podcasts:

1. Unchained by Laura Shin: Features interviews with industry leaders.

2. What Bitcoin Did by Peter McCormack: Explores Bitcoin-related topics.

YouTube Channels:

1. Andreas M. Antonopoulos: Renowned for his clear explanations of complex topics.

2. Coin Bureau: Known for deep dives into cryptocurrency projects.

7. Developer Documentation

For those interested in technical skills, official documentation is crucial:

Bitcoin Core Documentation: For developers who want to understand the Bitcoin protocol.

Ethereum Developer Documentation: A resource for building decentralized applications (dApps).

17.2. Staying Updated in a Rapidly Changing Field

The blockchain and cryptocurrency landscape changes daily, with new technologies, trends, and regulations emerging. Staying informed is essential for navigating this dynamic environment. Here's how to ensure you remain up to date:

1. Follow News Platforms

Stay tuned to reputable news outlets specializing in cryptocurrency and blockchain.

- **CoinDesk and CryptoSlate:** Offer daily updates on market trends and developments.
- **The Block:** Known for its deep industry analysis and reports.
- **Decrypt:** Features news and guides tailored to newcomers and experts alike.

Subscribing to newsletters like CoinDesk's Daily Update can deliver curated news directly to your inbox.

2. Leverage Social Media

Platforms like X formerly known as Twitter and LinkedIn are hotbeds for crypto news and discussions.

X: Follow thought leaders like Andreas M. Antonopoulos (@aantonop) and Vitalik Buterin (@VitalikButerin).

LinkedIn: Join professional groups focused on blockchain and cryptocurrencies.

YouTube: Many content creators provide weekly or daily updates.

However, always verify claims from social media to avoid misinformation.

3. Participate in Conferences and Meetups

Attending events is an excellent way to network and stay informed about innovations.

Major Conferences:

1. Consensus by CoinDesk: One of the largest blockchain events globally.

2. Blockchain Expo: Held in various locations annually.

3. Local Meetups: Platforms like Meetup.com list crypto and blockchain gatherings in your area.

Virtual conferences and webinars have also become popular, providing access to global experts from anywhere.

4. Monitor Regulations and Policies

Regulations vary across countries and can significantly impact the blockchain ecosystem.

- Follow updates from organizations like the Financial Action Task Force (FATF) and Securities and Exchange Commission (SEC).
- Websites like Coin Center provide insights into policy developments affecting cryptocurrencies.

5. Use Aggregator Tools

Information aggregators save time by collecting updates from multiple sources.

- **CryptoPanic:** Aggregates crypto news, updates, and market data.
- **Feedly:** Allows you to organize and follow RSS feeds from your favorite crypto blogs and news sites.

6. Join Professional Networks

Membership in blockchain associations can offer access to exclusive resources and industry updates.

- **Blockchain Association:** Provides insights into policy changes and advocacy efforts.
- **Enterprise Ethereum Alliance (EEA):** Focuses on blockchain applications in business.

7. Experiment with Tools and Technologies

Practical experience enhances theoretical knowledge.

Testnet Participation: Engage with blockchain testnets like Ethereum's Goerli to learn about smart contracts.

Wallets and Exchanges: Use crypto wallets like MetaMask and try trading on exchanges to gain hands-on experience.

8. Commit to Lifelong Learning

The crypto field demands continuous education. Consider:

Advanced Certifications:

- Certified Bitcoin Professional (CBP) by the CryptoCurrency Certification Consortium.
- Certified Blockchain Expert (CBE) by the Blockchain Council.

University Programs: Institutions like MIT, Stanford, and the University of Nicosia offer blockchain-specific courses.

9. Stay Skeptical and Verify Information

The decentralized nature of cryptocurrencies makes it prone to misinformation and scams. Always cross-check facts using multiple reliable sources.

10. Develop a Routine for Updates

Set aside dedicated time each week to catch up on crypto news, read articles, or explore new tools.

Building and maintaining expertise in Bitcoin, blockchain, and cryptocurrencies requires a combination of reliable resources, consistent updates, and hands-on experience. By leveraging the tools and strategies outlined in this chapter, you can stay ahead in this fast-paced field and position yourself as a knowledgeable participant in the decentralized future.

Conclusion

As we stand at the crossroads of technological evolution, Bitcoin and blockchain technology are reshaping the way we think about money, trust, and the very structure of our society. Since Bitcoin's emergence in 2009, blockchain technology has become a foundational innovation that extends far beyond digital currencies, promising a future that is decentralized, transparent, and more inclusive. This conclusion reflects on how blockchain is transforming the world and outlines steps to prepare for the decentralized future that lies ahead.

How Blockchain Is Transforming the World

Blockchain technology is no longer confined to the realm of cryptocurrencies. Its revolutionary potential lies in its ability to provide a secure, transparent, and decentralized ledger for virtually any type of data or transaction. Across industries and sectors, blockchain is driving innovation and addressing long-standing inefficiencies.

1. Financial Services and Inclusion

Blockchain is radically transforming financial services by providing secure, low-cost solutions for transactions, lending, and remittances. Cryptocurrencies like Bitcoin have enabled borderless, peer-to-peer transfers without the need for intermediaries such as banks. This innovation is particularly significant in regions with limited access to traditional banking systems, where blockchain can provide financial inclusion to billions of unbanked and underbanked individuals.

Smart contracts, a feature of blockchain platforms like Ethereum, are automating complex financial agreements, reducing the need for costly intermediaries and mitigating human error. Decentralized finance (DeFi) takes this a step further by offering loans, investments, and savings accounts in a trustless, permissionless environment.

2. Supply Chain Transparency

In global supply chains, blockchain is solving age-old problems of fraud, inefficiency, and lack of traceability. Companies can now track goods from origin to consumer, ensuring authenticity and reducing counterfeiting. For instance, the food industry is using blockchain to monitor the journey of produce, giving consumers confidence in their food's safety and origin.

Blockchain also provides a platform for ethical practices, enabling businesses and consumers to verify that products are sourced responsibly, whether it's fair-trade coffee or conflict-free diamonds.

3. Governance and Voting Systems

Transparent governance and tamper-proof voting systems are other areas where blockchain is making an impact. Blockchain-based voting can ensure fair elections by eliminating fraud and providing an immutable record of votes. In governance, decentralized autonomous organizations (DAOs) are exploring ways to manage communities and organizations without central authority, giving all participants a voice in decision-making.

4. Healthcare and Data Privacy

The healthcare industry faces challenges related to fragmented data, inefficiencies, and privacy concerns. Blockchain offers secure, unified access to medical records, enabling healthcare providers to collaborate more effectively while preserving patient privacy. Moreover, pharmaceutical companies can use blockchain to ensure the integrity of their supply chains, combating counterfeit drugs.

5. Intellectual Property and Creative Rights

Blockchain's ability to create immutable records is empowering artists, musicians, and content creators by ensuring they retain ownership of their work and receive fair compensation. Non-fungible tokens (NFTs), for example, have opened new revenue streams for creators by allowing them to tokenize and sell digital art, music, and other intellectual property.

6. Energy and Sustainability

Blockchain is also playing a critical role in promoting sustainability. Peer-to-peer energy trading platforms enable households and businesses to buy and sell excess renewable energy, reducing waste and reliance on centralized utilities. Blockchain can track carbon credits and other environmental metrics, making it easier for organizations to meet sustainability goals.

7. Humanitarian Applications

From providing identity solutions for refugees to streamlining aid distribution in disaster-stricken areas, blockchain is being used to address some of the world's most pressing challenges. Its ability to create tamper-proof records ensures that humanitarian aid reaches the intended recipients and minimizes corruption.

Preparing for a Decentralized Future

The widespread adoption of blockchain technology signals a shift toward a more decentralized world, where power and control are distributed among individuals rather than concentrated in institutions. To thrive in this new era, individuals, businesses, and governments must take proactive steps to adapt and prepare.

1. Embracing Decentralization

Decentralization is not just a technological shift; it's a cultural and societal transformation. It challenges long-standing hierarchies and centralized systems, empowering individuals to take greater control over their finances, data, and decisions. Governments and institutions need to embrace decentralization as an opportunity to innovate rather than resist it as a threat.

For individuals, understanding how decentralized systems work—whether it's Bitcoin, DeFi, or DAOs—is crucial to making informed decisions and leveraging the opportunities they present.

2. Fostering Education and Awareness

Education is key to unlocking the full potential of blockchain and cryptocurrencies. As the technology evolves, it's essential for educational institutions, governments, and private organizations to provide accessible resources and training. This includes introducing blockchain concepts in schools, offering professional development programs, and creating public awareness campaigns to demystify the technology.

3. Building Robust Regulations

While blockchain thrives on decentralization, regulatory frameworks are necessary to protect consumers, prevent fraud, and ensure stability. However, these regulations must strike a balance—they should foster innovation rather than stifle it. Collaborative efforts between governments, industry leaders, and blockchain communities can help establish policies that encourage growth while addressing concerns around security, privacy, and compliance.

4. Investing in Blockchain Development

Governments and businesses must invest in blockchain research and development to stay competitive. This includes funding projects that explore new use cases, improving scalability and energy efficiency, and integrating blockchain with emerging technologies like artificial intelligence (AI) and the Internet of Things (IoT). By investing in infrastructure and talent, nations and organizations can position themselves as leaders in the decentralized economy.

5. Enhancing Security and Scalability

As blockchain adoption grows, so does the importance of addressing its challenges, such as security vulnerabilities and scalability issues. Developers are already working on solutions like layer-2 protocols and sharding to improve transaction speeds and reduce costs. Ensuring robust security measures will also be critical to building trust and encouraging widespread adoption.

6. Encouraging Collaboration

The decentralized future will require collaboration across sectors and borders. Blockchain's potential can only be fully realized through partnerships that bring together governments, businesses, academia, and civil society. Open-source development, shared research, and cross-border initiatives can accelerate the technology's evolution and adoption.

7. Staying Adaptable

Finally, preparing for a decentralized future requires adaptability. Blockchain technology is still in its infancy, and its trajectory will likely include unexpected challenges and opportunities. By staying informed and open to change, individuals and organizations can navigate this dynamic landscape and capitalize on its potential.

A Glimpse Into the Future

The road ahead for Bitcoin and blockchain is filled with promise and complexity. As these technologies continue to mature, they will redefine the way we interact with money, data, and each other. Imagine a world where financial systems are truly global and inclusive, where supply chains are fully transparent, and where individuals have unprecedented control over their identities and assets.

This decentralized future isn't without its challenges, from regulatory hurdles to technological limitations. However, the progress made over the past decade demonstrates that blockchain has the resilience and adaptability to overcome these obstacles.

In the end, Bitcoin and blockchain represent more than just technological innovations—they symbolize a paradigm shift. They challenge us to rethink traditional systems and envision a world where trust is built into the very fabric of our transactions and interactions.

For those who embrace this change, the possibilities are limitless. Whether you're an individual looking to invest, a developer seeking to innovate, or a policymaker aiming to regulate, the time to engage with blockchain is now. The decentralized future is coming—it's up to us to shape it into one that benefits all.

www.ingramcontent.com/pod-product-compliance
Lightning Source LLC
Chambersburg PA
CBHW071025240526
45469CB00006BD/2092